The History Of The Proms

Celebrating 100 Seasons

🐧 *Published by:*
CMM Publications,
P.O. Box 547, High Wycombe,
Buckinghamshire HP12 4JJ,
England.
Telephone: 0494 473069
Fax: 0494 536842

© 1994 CMM Publications. All written material in this publication is strictly copyright and all rights are reserved. No part of this publication may be reproduced or transmitted in any form or by any means, electronic or mechanical including photocopying, recording or by any information storage or retrieval system without written permission of the publisher.

Front Cover Photographs:
The Proms Photo: © Rex Features Ltd.
Henry Wood Photo: © Hulton Deutsch Collection Ltd.
This page: © Rex Features Ltd.

AVANT L'AMOUR

a heart made for love

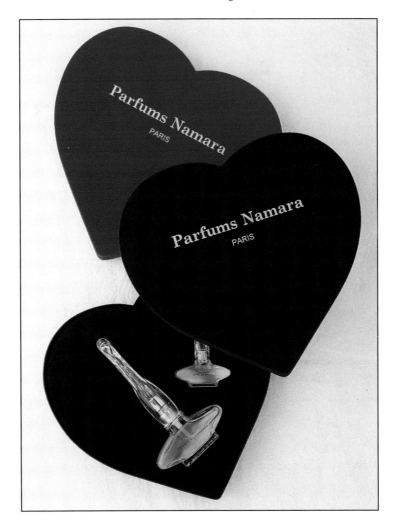

APRES L'AMOUR

a heart full of love

Available from all branches of

MAPPIN & WEBB

and

Watches *of* Switzerland

or telephone 0800 289 275

Introduction

T he book before you has been published so that a unique event in British musical history does not pass by undocumented. It's aim is to commemorate and celebrate the 100th Season of the Proms and also to revel in the history of the greatest music festival in the world.

I make no apologies for the anecdotal style in which it is written, as the purpose is not to produce an historic reference source, but to offer a thoroughly enjoyable read. To that end the combined use of graphics and photographs is employed in an attempt to 'bring to life' the events that occurred, in the hope that you, the reader, will be able to become involved and immersed in that history and for a while become part of the Proms themselves.

Numerous people are to be thanked for their help and never failing support, including AXA Equity & Law, whose policy to assist local businesses is greatly appreciated. This help has enabled an idea to become reality – to them I offer my sincere gratitude.

I hope this book goes some way to encapsulate the true spirit of the two originators, Robert Newman and Henry Wood.

Martin Chick
Publisher

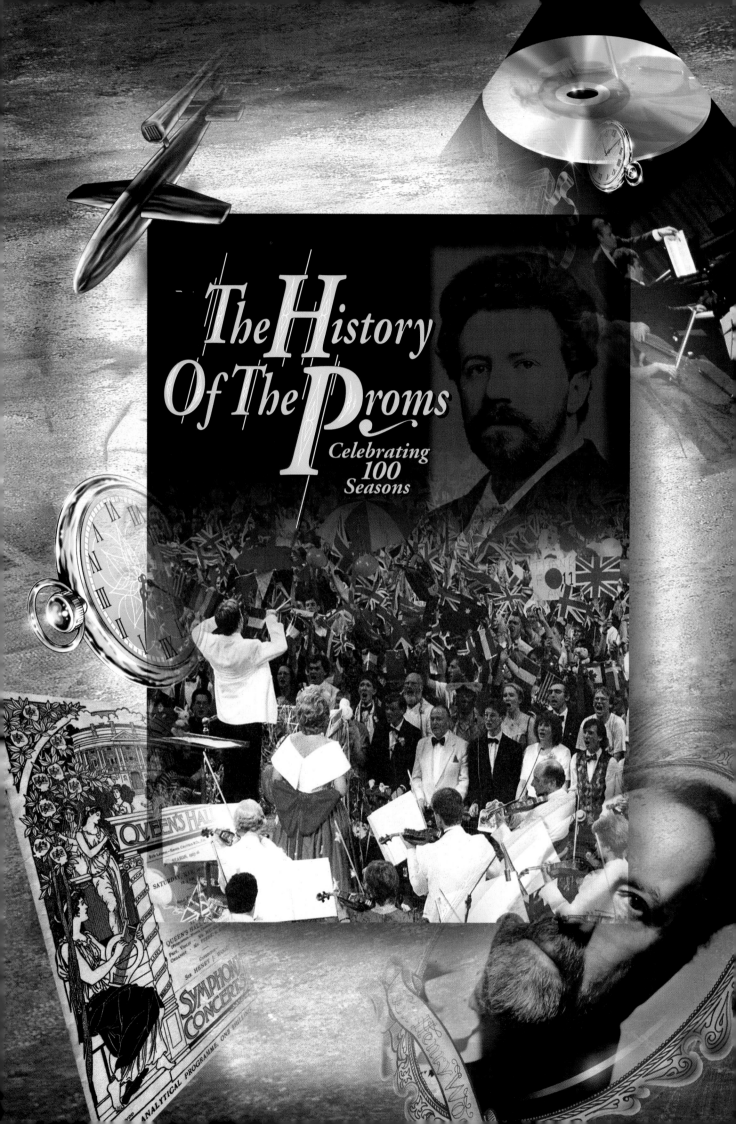

The History Of The Proms

Celebrating 100 Seasons

Foreword

by Henry Kelly

I am delighted to introduce this excellent book marking the 100th Season of the Henry Wood Proms. I suppose nearly everyone with even the slightest interest in and love of classical music will have a "Proms Story" of their own. Mine goes back more than 30 years to a young man - me and my father queuing in the early morning rain to get into the Albert Hall to hear a programme which included a Mozart piano concerto, a piece which I don't recall now but which I remember at the time making a mental note to forget, and the 1812 Overture. It was, looking back on it, just the type of evening's programme Henry Wood had in mind when he launched his wonderful venture with Robert Newman, so clearly detailed and reported in the following pages.

In his autobiography, *My Life of Music*, Wood recalls Newman telling him the year before the Proms started: "I am going to run nightly concerts and train the public by easy stages. Popular at first and gradually raising the standard until I have created a public for classical and modern music". It was and remains a noble aspiration whether for concerts or radio stations. For too long the great works of classical music seemed to be the preserve of the few. They belong to everybody who has an ear to listen and a mind to learn, yet if they are not made accessible, who but the elite can truly find their wonder?

Henry Wood's first Prom programme had a wide menu: from Wagner to Eckert, Leoncavello, Gounod, Bizet and Rossini. The programme that first evening had on its front page an advertisement from a firm of London tailors offering to make a suit for gentlemen lined throughout with silk for five guineas! I suppose that's one of the best indications of the durability of the whole venture.

Henry Wood and Robert Newman perhaps succeeded beyond even their own dreams in educating and entertaining the public by, as Wood put it, "interweaving novelties with the classics". To this day the Proms still do that. With the arrival of Classic FM in which I play my own daily part, the torch of passing on the great works of music to whoever wishes to hear them is carried a step further. Fortunately the sound of elitism, though not gone altogether from this land, is drowned out by the sounds of the world's most beautiful music. Sir Henry Wood started an unstoppable wave when he took the platform that evening, August 10th, 1895, at eight o'clock, to what he described as "a welcome that will always remain green in my memory". Long may the Proms continue for, though London-based, they have a national and international appeal. I am happy to be associated, in even the smallest way with a book which does so much to make permanent the work of great men.

Henry Kelly

Aldgate to Alwyn,
Brixton to Britten,
Croxley to Copland,
Dagenham to Delius,
Ealing to Elgar,
Fairlop to Franck,
Greenford to Grieg,
Hampstead to Haydn,
Ickenham to Ives,
Kilburn to Khachaturian,
Leyton to Liszt,
Morden to Mozart,
Neasden to Nielsen,
Ongar to Offenbach,
Poplar to Puccini,
Ruislip to Ravel,
Stratford to Strauss,
Temple to Teleman,
Victoria to Vivaldi,
Watford to Walton,

Take note!

You can't beat the Tube

UNDERGROUND

Contents

Publisher: *Martin Chick*
Editor: *Shirley Chick*
Writer/Research: *Peter Mullen*
Picture Research: *Pik Pooh*
Design and Illustration: *Joe Furey, Profile Direct Marketing Services Ltd. Tring, Herts.*
Electronic Image Manipulation: *Profile Direct Marketing Services Ltd. Tring, Herts.*
Reproduction: *Profile Direct Marketing Services Ltd. Tring, Herts.*
Advertising: *Chick Media & Marketing, High Wycombe, Bucks.*
Printing: *B.P.C. Waterlow Ltd.*
Special Thanks: *AXA Equity & Law, High Wycombe, Bucks.*

*The Publishers are unable
to accept, and hereby expressly
disclaim any liability for the
consequences of any inaccuracy,
errors or omissions in such
information, whether occurring
during the processing of
such information
for publication
or otherwise.*

Robert Newman
Lessee and Manager of
Queen's Hall and co-founder
with Henry Wood of the
Promenade Concerts

The Beginning of The Proms

"In those days musical performances were not so much feasts for the ear alone as all round entertainments. People went to see concerts as well as to hear them."

© Hulton Deutsch Collection Ltd.

*Exterior Sketch of
Queens Hall, 1930*

In the Marylebone Gardens behind the Rose of Normandy tavern you could get breakfast at 5 a.m. with fruit pies and cakes. In the same venue in the evenings you might hear a pipe-organ or opera extracts and you would almost certainly be treated to a fireworks display. This was in the middle of the eighteenth century and it is one of the earliest examples of Promenade concerts in Britain.

'Promenade' refers to walking, of course, and there is a long tradition of walking-around concerts in this country. Even in the 16th and 17th centuries the parks and gardens of London were full of buskers and acrobats and jugglers. Members of the public would pause to look and laugh - perhaps even to listen a while - and then continue their promenade. It was all highly informal - passing entertainment in the literal sense of the phrase.

But it was the eighteenth century - 'the age of elegance and proportion' - which saw the appointment of pleasure gardens for the purpose of outdoor performances. In 1730, for example Jonathan Tyers leased the Vauxhall Gardens and built a grandstand for the audience. Tyers was a man of unrestrained ambition who hired the best singers, recruited a large orchestra and engaged Thomas Arne (1710-78) as composer-in-residence. Arne was a writer of popular operettas such as *Rosamond* and *Tom Thumb* but his link with the Promenade concerts of today is as composer of *Rule Britannia.*

In those days musical performances were not so much feasts for the ear alone as all round entertainments. People went to see concerts as well as to hear them. For instance, on 21st April 1749 the public was invited to a pandemonic full dress rehearsal of Handel's *Music For The Royal Fireworks* and the spectacle, in keeping with the spirit of the age, was truly baroque, more like a circus than a symphony concert. Tyers hired Madame Saqui, the famous tightrope walker, who

walked the wire at an angle of sixty degrees *through* a display of fire-works. It was all enjoyed by the huge crowd to the accompaniment of vast quantities of food and drink. Not so much *se promener* as *manger.*

Rossini's enormous Parisian success *The Barber of Seville* was performed in the Vauxhall Gardens in 1829.

But as well as being the age of elegance and proportion, the eighteenth century was also a period of intense and fickle fashion. The public would, like the antihero of *Toad of Toad Hall,* be forever 'in the grip of a new craze.' In the 1750s the new craze in London was for ballooning, and alfresco musical jamborees were less favoured - so Tyers' emporium was closed down.

Even grander than the Vauxhall Gardens were those at Ranelagh which opened in 1742 with musical performances and a public breakfast, all for the price of two shillings (10p). It was a splendid place by all accounts, the sort of venue where Wagner's *Ring* might have been staged. There were canals and pleasure boats, Chinese buildings and a rococo rotunda 185 feet in diameter. Haydn played there. And on 28th June 1764 Leopold Mozart wrote to friends in Salzburg:

'On Friday 29th June, that is on the Feast of St. Peter and St. Paul, there will be a concert or benefit at Ranelagh in aid of a newly-established hospital and who ever wishes to attend must pay five shilling entrance. I am letting Wolfgang play a concerto on the organ at this concert in order to perform thereby the act of an English patriot who, as far as in him lies, endeavours to further the usefulness of this hospital which has been established for the public good. That is, you see, one way of winning the affection of this quite exceptional nation.'

The boy Mozart, aged eight, was billed in the official programme as 'the most extraordinary

prodigy and most amazing genius that has appeared in any age'. So we may confidently affirm that Mozart once played at an English Promenade Concert.

Regularly programmed at Ranelagh were works by Handel and Bach, Boyce and Arne and this goes to prove that, besides the pantomime aspects, good music did receive a hearing at the earliest Proms. Before Vauxhall or Ranelagh there was the opportunity to hear classical music played to a high standard in the capital, for example at the Hanover Square Rooms and at Hickford's Rooms. The Philharmonic Society - who introduced Beethoven's symphonies to England and sent the composer £100 when he was enduring his last illness - played at the Arghyll Rooms. But these concerts, at a guinea entrance fee, were beyond the reach of the ordinary people.

Philippe Musard (1793-1859) introduced Promenade concerts in Paris in 1833 and then in 1838 at Drury Lane where he advertised his 'mirrors, coaches, ottomans, statues, fountains and flowers.' There was also a rival series of concerts at the Crown and Anchor pub under Edward Eliason who also arranged performances at The Lyceum theatre in 1846.

The most popular musical - it can only be called 'phenomenon' - of the day was the quadrille. This was a sort of wild dance music first popular in France at the court of Napoleon I. It was brought to England by Lady Jersey, one of the leaders of fashion at the time, and at once it became a fad to the point of madness. Many composers wrote quadrilles based usually on popular songs. It was a square dance and it was in five movements, each movement of a different tempo. Sometimes in the early Promenade concerts the quadrilles were perfor- med with four or five military bands augmenting the orchestra. The enormous overkill and exaggeration was deliberately designed to create a sensation - a phenomenon. Musical

performances in those days were often akin to acrobatics.

The Crown and Anchor concerts were not small beer. The tavern had a hall which could hold 2,500 people and Eliason - an excellent violinist who had performed Beethoven's *Violin Concerto* - conducted Mozart's *Jupiter* Symphony there before a huge crowd.

The most famous of the nineteenth century musician-entertainers was Jullien. It would take too much space to give all his Christian names as there were a couple of dozen of them! He was named after all the members of the local philharmonic orchestra in the Alpine town of Sisteron where he was born in 1812.

Jullien was a character, larger than life, who even invented a kind of miraculous infancy for himself in the style of the heroes of classical Greece. It was said, for example, that he was snatched away by an eagle when he was no more than a toddler and that he cried from the earliest age at the sound of music: not because he was unmusical but because he was 'super-musical.' His perceptions were so refined, his senses so acute, that he had to be introduced to music only very gradually by successive approximation - rather in the same way that a nervous child is acquainted with a big fluffy dog.

Jullien was reputed to have been a fine singer in his early years, but he lost his voice (aged six!) and took up the violin. When he was fifteen he was wounded fighting for the French army at Navarino. After that he attended, for a time, Cherubini's harmony classes at the Paris Conservatoire but he was bored: 'Monsieur Cherubini, why can't I be allowed to compose dances as Mozart did?'

'Monsieur Jullien, you are like a woman who professes to become a nun but who all the time remains at her trade on the street.'

Jullien found the company of Rossini more congenial and the two men often ate together in the Paris cafes. He wrote quadrilles on popular French tunes of the day and played them at balls in Paris where he set off fireworks and fired cannons. At this time also he was involved in a duel as a consequence of an illicit love affair. He was pierced by his opponent's sword but he managed to pull it out, through the whole width of his body, to recover and to make his escape to England.

In 1840 he partnered Eliason in a short season of concerts from 8th July to 15th August at the Drury Lane theatre. There was an orchestra of ninety and a choir of eighty, a carpeted promenade, tropical plants and Beethoven's *Pastoral Symphony* was played with the additional scoring for the rattle of dried peas in a tin box - to 'authenticate' the storm scene! All this for a shilling (5p). Jullien was billed as 'the picturesque conducteur who is a whole gallery of pictures in his own person.' He also introduced the Polka to England and Queen Victoria did not approve - and she said as much.

Among all the barnstorming and the gimmicks the connection between the Proms of Jullien's day and those which were performed later under Newman and Henry Wood was the quality of the orchestral playing. Jullien behaved like a 1990s pop megastar but he was an accomplished musician himself; he knew the classics and he recruited the best musicians and paid well to keep them.

He mounted spectacular upon spectacular, the most extravagant of which was *The Destruction of Pompeii* which ended with 'the explosion of the crater, falling temples and the destruction of the city.' In 1845 he put on a five hundred piece orchestra at Covent Garden to play the *National Anthem* with a cannon shot in each bar. And he introduced his *Quadrille On British Sea Songs* which was a forerunner of Wood's.

© Hulton Deutsch Collection Ltd.

Interior of Queen's Hall, 1894

But in 1846 he played Mozart and Beethoven concerts and many musicians wrote years later in their memoirs that Jullien not only knew the classics better than most of his contemporaries but that he could also convey the spirit in which they should be played and so put them across to an audience. Jullien himself stated in 1850 his own aims in music: 'To ensure amusement as well as attempting instruction by blending in the programmes the most sublime works with those of a lighter school.' It might have been Henry Wood or Malcolm Sargent speaking.

He also composed *The Bloomers Quadrille* as a musical comment on a new style in ladies' underwear!

He performed oratorios by Mendelssohn as well as Handel's *Messiah* and *The Seasons* by Haydn. And he was an early champion of Wagner when that composer was almost universally despised among classical musicians. In 1860 Jullien died,

· QUEEN'S HALL, W. ·

Lessee and Manager   ROBERT NEWMAN.

PROMENADE CONCERTS

SEASON 1895

UNDER THE DIRECTION OF MR. ROBERT NEWMAN.

Programme for this Evening, Saturday, August 10th, 1895, at Eight o'clock.

DOORS OPEN AT **7** O'CLOCK EVERY EVENING.

MADAME MARIE DUMA.

MRS. VAN DER VEER-GREEN.

MR. IVER McKAY.

MR. W. A. PETERKIN.

MR. FFRANGCON-DAVIES.

MR. A. FRANSELLA.

Flute - MR. A. FRANSELLA.
Bassoon - MR. E. F. JAMES.
Cornet - MR. HOWARD REYNOLDS.

FULL ORCHESTRA.
Leader - - MR. W. FRYE PARKER.

ACCOMPANIST - MR. H. LANE WILSON.

Conductor = MR. HENRY J. WOOD.

PROMENADE OR BALCONY - ONE SHILLING.

GRAND CIRCLE SEATS (Numbered and Reserved) 2/6.

SEASON TICKETS (Transferable) ONE GUINEA.

No Charge for Booking Seats.

Seats Reserved the whole Evening.

FLORAL DECORATIONS BY MESSRS WILLS & SEGAR, ONSLOW CRESCENT, SOUTH KENSINGTON.

Theodore Nicholl,

ONLY AT

306, High Holborn.

SPÉCIALITÉ
EVENING DRESS.

**HIGH-CLASS
TAILORING**

AT

Moderate Charges.

THE SUIT (lined throughout silk) from **£5.**

SPATEN=BEER.

GABRIEL SEDLMAYR,
BRAUEREI ZUM SPATEN (MUNICH).
London Depot : 107, CHARING CROSS ROAD, W.C.

TO BE HAD AT THE BARS.

Supplied in Perfect Condition in Casks and Bottles from the above address

P.S.—Ask your Grocer for it.

For Advertisements on these Programmes application should be made to

CHARLES DEWYNTER, Limited.

Agents and Contractors for Advertisements,

23, HAYMARKET, LONDON, S.W.

Price Twopence.

manic-depressive and bankrupt. Hector Berlioz recalled in his memoirs how poor Jullien went mad in his last days: 'He would stick his fingers in his ears and, upon hearing the thunderous rush of blood, claim that he heard "Cosmic A", and Music of the Spheres.'

So, unhappily, perished a true pioneer of popular concerts.

Luigi Arditi (1822-1903) is nowadays perhaps best remembered for his Waltz *Il Bacio* - which was cruelly set to words advertising Ty-Phoo tea on Independent Television thirty years ago. But in 1875 and 1877 Arditi held a very successful series of Promenade concerts at Covent Garden. Wagner (in his own lifetime!) was all the rage.

The Liverpool Philharmonic Society was formed in 1840 and Charles Hallé (1819-95) - who was the first to play a Beethoven piano sonata in public in London - formed his orchestra in Manchester in 1856 where he kept prices to one shilling and received many delighted letters of appreciation from mill workers. Still, the working people were able to hear very little classical orchestral music or opera because affordable Promenade seasons came and went with fashion or endured until their proprietors wearied or went bankrupt. Such Proms as there were earned praise from George Bernard Shaw who, writing about musical life in London in the 1890s, described them as 'Beethoven to an accompaniment of popping corks. But, he said, 'you could have the run of the house for a shilling.' The most sustained attempt to perform good music at a reasonable price was made by August Manns who, between 1855 and 1901, conducted 20,000 afternoon concerts in winter at the Crystal Palace. His was the kind of example which Robert Newman desired above all to perpetuate.

Robert Newman was born in 1858 and he grew up to be a stockjobber and an amateur bass singer. His singing was rather better than the usual amateur, on account perhaps of his taking lessons in Italy while he was a young man. He was good enough, at any rate, to sing the title role in the first performance in the Oratorio *Job* by Hubert Parry. He was a hyperactive man with electric blue eyes. He said, 'I am going to run nightly concerts and train the public by easy stages. Popular at first, gradually raising the standard until I have created a public for classical and modern music.' Newman's determination was rewarded by a happy chance: it so happened that, at one and the same time, the ideal conductor and the perfect setting for these ambitions became available.

The old site of the Queen's Hall was by the Nash Church of All Souls, Langham Place - adjacent to the modern Broadcasting House. The land was Crown Property and many suggestions were put forward at the time of the Queen's Jubilee in 1887 as to what might most appropriately be built on it. A skating-rink was considered and rejected. At last it was decided to build a concert hall, designed mainly by the architect T.E. Knightley, a dour man with a wretchedly dull sense of what goes into a colour scheme but with a wonderful talent for constructing a building that turned out to be acoustically almost perfect: resonant but without the Royal Albert Hall's perplexing echo, and with no 'silent spots.' It was a popular venue from the first.

Newman became the first lessee of the Queen's Hall and its manager. He had heard Henry Wood, then a young man of twenty-four, play the organ accompaniment at the first concert ever played there, on 2nd December 1893. Wood described him thus: 'He was always brisk and busy but the moment he discussed music his blue eyes - they were *very* blue - lighted up as with fire, and the soft inner kindness of the man showed him to be a deep lover of music. He must have misled many by his abrupt manner, but once he spoke of art all that disappeared. He had plenty of experience in running Promenade concerts at His Majesty's, so that he knew what he was about.'

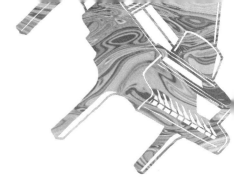

He had organised concerts on a Sunday afternoon and dealt diplomatically with the objections of the 19th century precursors of the 'Keep Sunday Special' movement! Those first meetings to arrange the Promenade concerts in the Queen's Hall are best described by the other man who was involved, Henry Wood himself:

'I did not meet him again until he called on me in February, 1895. With hardly a word of greeting he tackled the question of what was obviously uppermost in his mind. "I have decided to run those Promenade concerts I told you about last year. I want you to be the conductor of a permanent Queen's Hall Orchestra. We'll run a ten weeks' season."
'I can still feel the thrill of that moment. An orchestra ... in Queen's Hall ... *My* orchestra ...

'"But you have never seen me conduct."'

'"Oh yes I have! As often as I could - wherever you were. Given the right orchestra, you will become a *great* conductor. Anyhow, I mean to run you and *make* you. The public will support us. The time is ripe for an English conductor ... and now ... can you put up a little capital ... say two or three thousand pounds?"'

'I'm afraid not. I haven't such a sum to risk, and don't know anyone who has.'

'"Never mind! I'll see what can be done. *For I mean to run those concerts!*"'

Wood then ran off - we must imagine with wings on his heels - to give a singing lesson to a Scotsman called Peterkin who was accompanied by a friend who came to listen. At a break in the lesson, Wood told Peterkin of Newman's ambition, whereupon the man at the other end of the room - the man who had come to listen - said, 'Please tell me more about this project, Mr. Wood."
This man was Dr. George Cathcart, an ear and throat specialist. 'I want you to introduce me to Newman,' he said, 'I might put up the money if

he will do two things: one is to establish the *low pitch* and the other to engage you as his only conductor.'

Cathcart, as a throat specialist, knew what damage the English vogue for high pitch was having on singers' voices, whereas the lower pitch was the fashion on the continent. It was nearly impossible to sing oratorios in the high pitch and English singers were already protesting about this. Unfortunately for them, most English organs and wind instruments were pitched high so the singers were left with no choice but to strain their voices or go without employment.

Wood introduced Dr. Cathcart to Robert Newman: 'Newman *liked* the high pitch, but he succumbed to Dr. Cathcart's better judgement. Of what the financial arrangements were, I knew practically nothing. But I do know that Dr. Cathcart was directly responsible for the inception of the Promenade concerts in August 1895.'

When it comes to giving thanks for those who had the foresight and the generosity to embark on that first season of the Proms, the ear and throat surgeon, George Cathcart, should not be forgotten.

Newman undoubtedly had a genius for administration and one of his brightest insights was the provision of the one guinea (£1.05) transferable season ticket which was, as its name implies, for all the concerts. This represented amazing value for money in an age when a single ticket for a symphony concert might cost anything between five shillings (25p) and £1. In reality, Newman was a public benefactor succeeding brilliantly in his desire to provide the best of music at affordable prices in the days when financial distinctions in society were much greater than they are today.

The first season was a success and Newman was given a benefit concert at the end of it which

raised £400. The success was the result of imaginative programming, good orchestral playing and a realistic pricing system for admissions. Newman never let up in his efforts to ensure continued success. As Wood said, 'He always had an eye for the main chance. He would take advantage not only of any centenary but also of the demise of any public personage!'

Newman's business difficulties made it impossible for him to carry financial responsibility for the orchestra after 1901, but by this time the Promenade concerts were well-established and other men appeared on the scene to share the burden.

There is a note of sadness in all this inspired creative and imaginative activity, for Robert Newman seems almost to be the forgotten man in the history of the Proms. He does not receive many column inches in the musical histories of our time and he is missing altogether from the *Dictionary of National Biography* - even from the

supplements to that great work. Yet without Newman there would probably have been no Proms.

He died in 1926 and a memorial was placed in the Queen's Hall, a small plate behind the seat he usually took in the second circle. This was destroyed in the bombing of 1941. Wood wrote movingly of his impresario and friend:

'I always knew the state of the barometer with Newman from the habit he had of looking out of the corner of his eye while his moustache bristled fiercely. We never fell out.

'Dear Robert Newman whom I can still visualise with that bristling moustache and his blue eyes afire with enthusiasm that day in 1895 when he suggested I should direct Promenade concerts in the newly-built Queen's Hall.'

Queen's Hall, 1890

© Hulton Deutsch Collection Ltd

Sir Henry Wood

Henry Wood:

A Man with a Vision.

"There was never any doubt that he would make his presence felt in the world."

© Hulton Deutsch Collection Ltd.

From the moment when, aged two, Henry Joseph Wood, straining to get a better sight of a hurdy-gurdy man and his monkey, fell out of his baby chair and broke his nose, there was never any doubt that he would make his presence felt in the world.

He was born in 1869 in London, in Oxford Street where his father was an optician and a maker of model engines. H.J. Wood senior also played the cello, as his son tells us, ' with a less than perfect technique but a fine tone' and he gave young Henry every aid and encouragement to make his way in music. And not only in music but in art for, from an early age, Henry was a talented painter in water colours and in oils.

Young Wood's character, so soon established, suggests highly nervous perpetual motion. He rigged up a communications system of pipes between his own room and that of his parents but at night he stuffed a cork into his end of the pipe so that they wouldn't hear his insomniacal piano practice. Besides the piano, Henry kept white mice and a guinea pig in his bedroom as well as an Alexander harmonium purchased from Noel Coward's uncle. At junior school he won all the prizes going.

Biographers of Henry Wood stress his energy and his huge capacity for work, conjuring up the impression of one of his father's engines, all noise and steam and allegro molto. But he also had a developed sense of the absurd and an eye for life's more bizarre offerings, as for example in this description of an incident involving his music librarian Edmund Grist:

'Grist was a colourless man who rarely if ever smiled and certainly had no sense of humour. One day a telegram arrived, addressed to me at Queen's Hall. It was from Tosta de Benici, the well-known Swedish pianist, who was to appear at a Promenade Concert. It read: TELL CHRIST TO PUT OUT THE BAND PARTS OF THE GRIEG CONCERTO. I handed it to Grist - who read it, and turned to me without the trace of a smile: " She's spelt my name wrongly - it's not Christ, it's Grist".'

For a while he attended St. John's Wood Art School as a pupil and here too he was quick to scorn pretentiousness. A girl student who thought rather too well of herself was challenged by Whistler (who happened to be paying a visit): 'Don't you think you've painted too much green under that man's arm?'
Not at all. I always paint what I see.'
Wood records with glee Whistler's reply, turning away, sotto voce,
'God help her when she sees what she's painted!'

With even more glee Wood recalls how he 'ran away' from the Royal Academy of Music disgusted because the Principal had delegated an incompetent student to conduct him (Wood) in an organ concerto: 'I received two bronze and two silver medals during my two years at the RAM, but I did not return after this incident.'

He was precocious - he accompanied services on the church organ almost before his feet could reach the pedals - and conceited: 'When I was organist at St. John's Fulham I improved the quality of the singing enormously.' He records how almost everyone he met praised him, including Sir Arthur Sullivan - 'who asked my advice' - and Ruskin, 'who looked at me with an air of interest.'

To read Wood's autobiography *My Life of Music* is to get the impression of one who never doubted, even as a child, that he was destined to take his place in the Pantheon. But his self-confidence, which otherwise might have become overbearing, is mitigated by his sense of self-mockery - as when he recalls his gaffe of playing a funeral march by mistake at a wedding. And the vivid, painter's perception never dimmed: Wood

describes a singer as having 'eyelashes like the railings in Hyde Park.'

He made a good living in his teens as a singing teacher but in addition to this there was always his father in the background providing for him, furthering his musical education by paying for him to travel, even as far as Boston in the USA, to hear the world's finest orchestras and meet the great conductors. Was he privileged to meet them or they him? He recalls, 'I met the great Felix Mottl who liked me and took a great interest in my conducting of Wagner.' Wood was seventeen at the time; Mottl was conducting the Bayreuth Festival!

Wood's first regular employment as a conductor was with The Arthur Rousbey Grand English Opera Company which was really no more than a glorified touring concert party. They opened in Rochdale with *Don Giovanni* only to discover they had no horse for the Commendatore's graveyard scene in the second act. They sent to Middlesborough to borrow a pantomime cow which they cut about a bit and affixed a bicycle saddle - it was that sort of opera company. Wood was underpaid and overworked. He retired exhausted and returned to teaching singing, this time in partnershp with his friend Gustav Garcia.

His next conducting arrangement was to accompany the popular favourite soprano Marie Roze's farewell tour with the Carl Rosa Opera Company. This was a much happier experience. Wood records: 'I had many happy hours with this radiant personality. One night, after a perfectly terrific stagedoor demonstration, the crowds practically lifted Marie into her carriage. As soon as we were inside, she made me pull down the blinds and, in order to get away at all, I waved my hand from underneath the blind and had it shaken and kissed by the excited crowd who doubltess thought it was hers!'

When Wood was twenty-five, his father gave up his business to become his son's full-time secretary and the family moved house to 1 Langham Place - right beside the newly built Queen's Hall. Shortly after this, Wood met Robert Newman and the rest is history - or rather, a living legend.

In 1896, the year after the first opening of the Proms, Henry Wood's mother died. He was distraught and he later said of her, 'My mother was my home - and almost my music too.' His grief was sincere and profound and yet there is something in Wood's own account of the event and the hours that followed which is almost surreal:

'In February my mother died suddenly of bronchitis. I shall always remember the kindness of my friend Joseph O'Mara that night. I was beside myself in my agony of loss but, incongruous as it may seem, I gained comfort from his taking me out to Romano's and making me eat a few oysters.'

There is no doubt that his enduring comfort was not oysters but music in general and the Promenade Concerts in particular which by this time had become his whole life. Henry Wood *was* the Proms. But he was still only twenty-seven and old orchestral hands sometimes gave him a hard time, one violinist asking in far from hushed tones and in the conductor's earshot, 'I wonder where Newman picked up this brat Wood?'

His fastidiousness riled the players on occasions. For example, he was a great one for precise pitch and every player had to file past him in tune. For this purpose he devised a piece of apparatus worked by a handle on the principle of an organ pipe. It had a small wind chest containing three sets of bellows, each of which relieved the next as they successively ran out of breath. It remained absolutely in tune for years and it is widely known that the players hated it.

Wood lived in Langham Place with his father and they were looked after by a series of housekeepers, none of whom were entirely satisfactory. At the time, Wood was teaching singing to Princess Olga, the beautiful daughter of Princess Sofie Ouroussoff of Podolia, Russia, and he confided in his pupil his dissatisfaction with the housekeepers: 'I asked Olga whether she considered my housekeeper could manage on less than £14 a week and learned to my surprise that half this sum would, or should, suffice. However,' he adds 'it was our music that drew us together.'

They were married in 1898 and, as Wood wrote, 'We spent a glorious six weeks at Braemar even though it rained the whole time.' At this time Wood's father moved away to live with his son's pupil and friend Ben Grove.

When Wood was not conducting a concert - either at the Proms or at a provincial music festival or on a foreign tour - he was to be found rehearsing a concert or else giving a singing lesson: he was accustomed to give five hundred or more such lessons every year. He wrote, 'Olga never permitted anything of a domestic nature to interfere with my music.'

But there was no life outside music for either of them. Wood said, 'There *could* have been a perpetual round of social pleasures. The temptation to accept some of the invitations we received was indeed great, but we had to risk offending people - even to forgoing all the pleasures of parties and country house weekends. We got to bed as early as possible.' There is not even a hint in Wood's tone of regret for these social omissions.

There was one supreme social occasion around this time when Wood was presented to Queen Victoria, who was then eighty after a concert he had conducted at Windsor Castle. He relished the occasion except for the fact that he was required to wear white kid gloves for the performance and he recalls, 'I felt like a bandmaster at a seaside pier.' The Queen was delighted with the concert but there was an awkward moment afterwards when she enquired. 'Tell me, Mr. Wood, are you quite English? Your appearance is - er - rather un-English!' Perhaps it was the beard?

Wood's practice of including works in all his concerts by living composers meant that he came into daily contact with those whom we now know as household names: Elgar, Delius and Richard Strauss; Debussy, Holst and Vaughan Williams. In fact in the early days of the Proms, Wood had Gustav Holst in his orchestra, as a trombonist: 'He looked so ill I told him to go to Margate for a week's rest.' It is not known whether the future composer of *The Planets* took the confident young conductor's advice.

He fell out with Debussy over fees, offering the French master only a hundred guineas - later upped to two hundred. And in 1902 he took Richard Strauss' wife shopping for knickers in Regent Street. There is a moving account in a letter to Wood from Lord Chandos, of how the great Polish pianist Paderewski had asked to be introduced to Wood's father:

'Your father told me that after one of the concerts at Queen's Hall in which you had conducted for Paderewski, who after saying nice things to you upon the performance, said he had been told that your father was present in the hall and that he would like to meet him. So they sent for him and Paderewski took him by the hand and said how honoured and pleased he was to meet him, and congratulated him upon having such a son.

'When telling me this, tears were in your father's eyes at the memory because, as he said, "Of all the great artists appearing at Queen's Hall, possibly not one ever gave a thought

© Hulton Deutsch Collection Ltd./CMM Publications

or wondered whether you ever *had* a father - except Paderewski, the greatest of them all".' The anecdote is a reminder both of Paderewski's graciousness and Henry Wood's youthfulness.

In 1902 Wood was again exhausted and ill, and on doctor's orders he went on a cruise to Morocco - without Olga. While he was away, his father died. Wood did not return but stayed with the cruise as scheduled. When the ship eventually approached Liverpool, the port was under a fog and they were unable to dock. Wood was greatly agitated for he had a rehearsal the next day. So he begged the captain to let him off down the rope ladder by night and on to a tug. All this was accomplished under darkness and Wood then dashed by train to the Queen's Hall where he had a rehearsal at half past two in the afternoon. It sounds odd, then, when you hear Wood saying a few years later: ' The American method of living at top speed and white heat cannot be successfully applied to art.'

In the last concert of the 1909 season on 23rd October, Olga sang three of Delius' songs, the third of which ended with the words, 'In love's white flame, in love's transcendent light.' Olga died on 20th December. She had been ill some years and had never fully recovered. Wood wrote:

'Her passing left a greater blank than that of even my dear mother in that I had now lost a comrade and the love of my life. I felt that life for me was now devoid of all meaning. It is not often given man and woman to find such a perfect union as ours had been, for Olga was so much the embodiment of all I ever wanted musically and artistically, coupled with a worldly sophistication with which her upbringing had endowed her (and which was so lacking in me) that she was able to help me form plans for a future I could never have conjured up for myself at that time.'

He adds her epitaph: *'In love's white flame ... in love's transcendent light'* and recalls that he cannot remember conducting concerts immediately afterwards - on Boxing Day and on New Year's Day . *'I notice that I conducted two concerts,'* he writes distractedly.

In 1911, at the age of 42, Wood was knighted 17 years after conducting his first Proms concert. Whilst the Knighthood meant so much to him, his despair that Olga was not with him to share it was obvious.

In his autobiography Wood takes candour to the edge of rashness on occasions and generally he does not spare the reader a 'warts and all' presentation of himself, but on one event he is quite amazingly silent: his marriage in 1911 to his secretary Muriel Ellen Greatrex, daughter of Major Ferdinand William Greatrex of the First Royal Dragoons. Wood was exactly twice Muriel's age.

Almost from the start they were incompatible perhaps mainly because Muriel was not content, or perhaps able, to organise the whole domestic scene which, in Olga's day, had been the secure background to Wood's hectic musical activities. After a few years the wear and tear of this incompatibility began to show as Wood became frequently irritable, untidy and even below par in matters of personal hygiene. The orchestral players murmered, affectionately employing their conductor's nickname, 'What's the matter with Old Timber?'

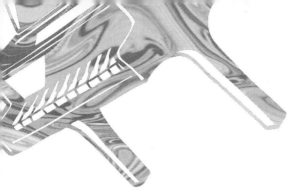

In 1934 Wood suffered a slight heart attack and he was desperate for a companion to help him in his recovery, to provide that personal warmth which had been missing from his life since Olga's death. He renewed his acquaintance with Jessie Linton who had just been widowed. It was almost as if he threw himself on her mercies, imploring her to rescue him from his dejection and the debilitating disorder which his life had become. She became his music manager and agent and quickly discovered that, outside music, his practical competence was nil. Very soon his colleagues were remarking that Old Timber looked ten years younger and that he was back to his amiable self again. Jessie took the title 'Lady Wood' by deed poll because his wife had refused to divorce him and thenceforth she was always on hand to deal with his domestic and professional needs, some of which required a woman's tact.

For example, the celebrated harpist Sidonie Goossens recalled, 'He was in favour of women in the orchestra, as everyone knows. But he didn't like lady cellists: they showed far too much leg for his taste. So he sent Lady Wood to tell women players to please cover up.'

Wood's stamina was legendary. There were six concerts each week of the Promenade Season and he conducted them all. These concerts had to be planned, arranged and rehearsed. On top of all this there was the entertaining of international musical celebrities to be managed - Mrs. Strauss' knickers expedition!

This regime was necessary for his stamina and he complained when provincial impresarios told him airily that he could *easily* catch a train back home to London ten minuted after the end of a concert. 'Ten minutes!' retorted Wood 'I perspire profusely and it would be suicidal to start on a journey without a change and a rub-down.'

He had been something of an athlete in his time: 'At any rate I was keen enough to cycle from Nottingham to London, a distance of a hundred and twenty-five miles in one day.'

The relentless, frenetic activity, the high-seriousness of Wood's passion for standards in orchestral rehearsal and playing, his meticulous attention to correspondence - all these things suggest a man of punctilious efficiency and supreme reliability. But he was a humorous man with a good ear not just for absolute musical pitch but a joke. Above all, he enjoyed the comedy of situations and this prompts the thought that, had he not spent almost all his life producing orchestral music, he would have been an excellent director of opera.

Wood's anecdotes about legendary composers and performers in the most unlikely or comic situations are superb. He recalls, 'A man came to repair my bicycle. I saw him leaning over the piano and looking out of the window. He had his back to me and I noted his wide breeches which were not unlike plus fours. "Thank you for calling so promptly," I began "I want you to look at my bicycle."

'The figure at the piano turned round" "Bicycle? I am Ethel Smyth!"' (the great operatic composer and feminist).

© Hulton Deutsch Collection Ltd.

On another occasion Wood had to entertain the composer Max Reger - 'one of the greatest contrapuntists of modern times' - to lunch before a performance of Reger's *Serenade* at the Proms:

'Knowing nothing of his likes and dislikes, I took the precaution of ringing up the German Club. They told me I must order in at least a couple of dozen bottles of beer.

'Never shall I forget the appearance in our dining-room with all these bottles in a row. The lunch began at one but it did not end until half past three when we retired to the drawing-room. Although the good Reger had lived up to his reputation and had consumed most of the beer without the slightest inconvenience to himself, I thought the poor fellow might be thirsty so I offered him a whisky and soda. He was so pleased with the first that he had three more. He did not, however, remain to tea. He drove to the German Club after leaving us. I told Olga I thought he had gone down there to get a drink.'

Orchestral players found it easy, now and then, to mock Wood's bustling seriousness, as in the case of the little bell which he always kept by him on the music stand and which he would ring to catch musicians' attention: 'Hot water please for all in room number seven!' was a favourite cry. But Wood's basic generosity of spirit was never in doubt and he was, after all, sympathetic to bad playing. He would sigh and say, 'Poor darlings, they're all worried.' He mounted an exhibition of his sketches in oil in 1911 and the proceeds were given to musicians' charities. He said, 'I am proud of having raised the weekly wage of orchestral musicians.'

And he would sometimes tell stories against himself to musicians 'after hours'. One of his favourites was of a little boy outside the concert hall with his uncle: Uncle: "Now come along, we are going in to hear Mr. Wood and his lovely orchestra."

'Little boy: "But I don't want to hear Mr. Wood. I want to go on the scenic railway!"'

He was not the century's finest conductor and he would never have claimed that position for himself but, in a lecture in 1905, Elgar described Wood as 'the only English conductor - a giant.' Victor Gollancz wrote perceptively, 'No one could have called him a great conductor, but he carried usefulness to the point of genius.'

No one, that is, except his audiences. They loved him. Even small children had heard of the great conductor. Wood himself tells the story of the Rector of Coningsby who had been giving his children a talk about the Patron Saint of Music, St. Cecilia. 'Now,' said the Rector 'who *is* the Patron Saint of Music?'

'Please Sir, I know - Sir Henry Wood!'

The audiences adored him and he, for the most part, adored his audiences though he could speak his mind when he was roused: 'Saturday afternoon concerts were often full of the gossipy type of women season-ticket holders whom one sees at seaside orchestral concerts and who knit,

© BRITISH BROADCASTING CORPORATION

talk and sew the whole time ... Once in a quiet interlude in Tchaikovsky's Fifth, a voice from such an audience piped up, "Oh no, we always fry ours in drippin'!"'

He also said, 'It distresses me sometimes when I look round the audiences at symphony concerts to note how comparatively few people take the trouble to dress; whereas everyone dresses for the opera.'

Despite these occasional criticisms, Wood had an abiding respect for those who came to listen night after night and he would often defend the Prommers' taste against the sneering attitude of musical snobs: 'I extracted a certain amount of private delight and reassurance from the fact that several ultra-modern works this season were hissed in no unmistakable manner. It gave me enormous satisfaction to realise that the audience was not composed of passive listeners but of a public capable of expressing their judgment.'

And he added, 'I maintain that the public knows - and must be given - what it wants. For saying which I need not be deemed old fashioned or unprogressive. For no conductor can have produced more contemporary works than I.' Indeed he was right in that assessment. Almost every concert contained new works - 'novelties', as he called them - alongside old favourites. It was this mastery of the art of programming which caused Ethel Smyth - herself a rigorous modernist - to exclaim, 'It was generous-minded Sir Henry Wood who first started mixed-bathing in the sea of music.' That remark also applied to Wood's encouragement of women orchestral players.

In return the audiences cheered him until the roof nearly blew off and never more loudly than on 11th October 1912 when Wood's transport crashed in the fog and he entered twenty minutes late with his head bandaged. This was the only time in his career that he was late for a performance. For a few days that accident forced him to modify his regime which was: bed at one o'clock in the morning; cold bath at half past six; an hour of score-reading before breakfast.

1938 marked Wood's Jubilee as a conductor and Rachmaninov came on 5th October to play his *C minor concerto* at a commemorative concert. Typically, Wood gave the proceeds to endow nine beds for musicians in six London hospitals. He was summoned to three encores and finally the only way he could make his escape was by a burlesque: he returned to the platform wearing his overcoat; then a second time adding a scarf; at last in his gloves and hat as well.

Wood was thrilled by his Jubilee celebrations and he took a child-like delight in the acclaim and festivities: 'I shopped all morning. Nothing gives me more pleasure than a visit to our fine London shops. Ties, shoes, ordering a fresh supply of cigars and cigarettes and my one vice - glacé stem ginger!'

There was a surprise party for Sir Henry's Jubilee to surpass anything that subsequently appeared on TV's *This Is Your Life*. He imagined he was on his way to a simple lunch with his young friend Dr. Calthrop when he heard, coming from the dining-room, the strains of Bach's *Toccata and Fugue in D minor* - 'excellently played too', as he remarked at the time.

It turned out to be his own recording of that dramatic work. He was shown into a room lit by sixty-nine birthday candles which he first counted and then blew out one by one. Later there was a splendid dinner at Quaglino's and the toast was 'Sir Henry: your sixty-ninth birthday!'

He replied: 'I cannot believe it. I still do not feel a day over fifty and am good for ... well, you never know! After all, did not Verdi write *Falstaff* at eighty and the *Te Deum and Stabat Mater* at eighty-five? Tintoretto painted *Paradiso*, a canvas measuring seventy-four by thirty feet, at seventy-

four; Goethe completed *Faust* at eighty; Cato began to learn Greek at the same age; Tennyson wrote *Crossing the Bar* at eighty-three ... Titian painted that wonderful historic canvas *The Battle of Lepanto* at ninety-eight. So what is a mere sixty-nine?'

It was a bravura performance but the very fact that Wood had apparently mugged up on all these venerable artists in order to reel off their latter-day achievements sounds a little like an essay in self-encouragement, if not in self-deception. Did he have an inkling that he himself might not last as long as, say, Titian or Goethe?

At any rate he cut down his activities at least a little. From 1941 Wood agreed to share the burden of conducting all the Proms with Basil Cameron. Lady Wood, among others began to be concerned about his health and she wrote in 1943, 'There was a veiled touchiness that was new to him and betokened weariness of the spirit.'

At the beginning of the forty-ninth season (1943) he almost collapsed in front of six thousand people while conducting Brahms' *Second Symphony*. His own puzzled comment on the incident was: 'Damn silly - I've tried to keep upright - can't understand it - had to beat almost below the desk.' What he could not, or would not understand, was that sixty years and more of ceaseless activity, of intellectual and emotional involvement at the highest level were making inroads into his constitution and his resources of stamina. All men are mortal.

Also, volumes could be written in amplification of Lady Wood's remark about his weariness of spirit. For Wood had not only programmed, arranged, rehearsed and performed the world's greatest series of symphony concerts for half a century, he had also had to deal with a great deal of attrition, of sheer wear and tear

© Hulton Deutsch Collection Ltd./CMM Publications

along the way: all that wrangling with the BBC over finance, venues and personalities when all Sir Henry wished to do was conduct!

He had a month in bed and then returned, as Lady Wood said, 'Alive again. The old fire returned, glowing throughout the remaining concerts.' The Proms attendances for that 1943 season exceeded a quarter of a million, a record and, for the first time, Wood let children into the rehearsals. There was a valedictory tone, a palpable mellowing.

On 3rd March 1944, Wood celebrated his seventy-fifth birthday and a national Jubilee fund was set up under Lord Horder: 'To mark an epoch in English music and to provide a new and much needed concert hall in central London to hold four thousand people.'

King George VI sent his congratulations saying, 'You are the nation's greatest teacher of music.' His friends at the Savage Club invented a rhyme:

'A hundred seasons may elapse
Ere timber reach its prime;
Small wonder then we hope our Wood
Will go on beating time.'

Sir Arthur Bliss composed a fanfare. The Poet Laureate, John Masefield, wrote a commemorative poem. It was not, it must be said, his best. Indeed an unkind critic described it as, 'Tripe and rather cold tripe at that.' The last lines were:
'Lord of sweet music and of Langham Place,
Today this nation thanks and praises you.'

The Daily Telegraph sponsored a concert in the Royal Albert Hall which was graced by the attendance of the Queen and the young princesses, Elizabeth and Margaret.

In July, Wood was behaving strangely again, as he had done the year before and astonishingly, breaking a lifelong rule, he cancelled a full rehearsal of Beethoven's *Seventh Symphony* before the concert on 28th July. Jessie asked him why he should, so late in the day, alter his usual practice, his golden rule. He replied, 'But you watch. Tonight I will *make* them play it!' He did not want to be left alone in the afternoon so his wife stayed with him. He slept restlessly. Wood's biographer, Reginald Pound, describes the concert:

'That night the note of genial rapport was missing. "Now!" he was heard to say fiercely under his breath, and he raised the baton for the heavy opening chords that lead into the oboe melody of the introduction to the *Seventh*

© BRITISH BROADCASTING CORPORATION

Symphony. The frenetic vitality of the *Scherzo* and *Trio* and the *Finale*, called from him his last reserve of psychic power.

'He "made them play" superbly well according to some practised listeners, who might all too appositely have described it as a monumental performance. He conducted the symphony like a natural force finally and inexorably expending itself. Within a few hours of returning to the hotel after the concert, he was in the throes of another terrible rigor.'

Wagner once referred to Beethoven's *Seventh Symphony* as 'the apotheosis of the dance.' For Wood it was the dance of death. He recovered. He was awarded the *Companion of Honour* by the King but he was too ill even to listen to the Proms anniversary concert on the radio on 10th August. Sir Adrian Boult sent him a note: 'Here we all are, audience, orchestra, announcer, soloists and conductor, waiting to begin your Jubilee celebration, and very sad that you are not with us. We all send our love and wish you a quick recovery, and many more Proms to come!'

He died on 19th August and his ashes were interred at the Church of St. Sepulchre, Holborn Viaduct where he had played the organ in the 19th Century as a boy.

In that century, Britain was ridiculed on the continent as 'the land without music'. In fifty years, Sir Henry Wood first created and then developed and educated the biggest and the most enthusiastic and sophisticated audience for music in the world. As George Bernard Shaw said, 'It was Wood who dragged British orchestral music alive out of the abyss.' The whole nation, in spirit if not in the flesh, attended his funeral.

He could be hasty in his judgments and sometimes so full of himself and his preoccupations that orchestral players were forced to laugh at his idiosyncracies and his high

© Hulton Deutsch Collection Ltd.

'My dear Promenaders.'

seriousness - so high it could be comical. But his mission was never in doubt and that was, as he proclaimed in his manifesto with Robert Newman back in 1895, 'to run nightly concerts and train the public by easy stages. Popular at first, gradually raising the standard until I have created a public for classical and modern music in this country.'

Perhaps the greatest tribute which can be paid to him is that in all his blaze of activity he never forgot to be kind. He gave of himself, not merely of his considerable talent. Denis Matthews, the celebrated musician, wrote while he was only a schoolboy to Wood, thanking him for a particular performance and asking a few questions about music. Wood replied in his own hand and enclosed a bundle of gramophone records and a new textbook on harmony. As Matthews asked, 'how could such a famous and busy conductor find time to care for an unknown young admirer?'

He cared for them all, and especially for ***'My dear Promenaders.'***

QVEEN'S HALL

Sole Lessees—Messrs. CHAPPELL & Co., LTD.

3 SEASON, 1925-26.

SATURDAY, MAR. 20TH, 1926,
AT 3 P.M.

SOLO PIANOFORTE—
CORTOT.

THE NEW
QUEEN'S HALL ORCHESTRA
(Proprietors—Messrs. CHAPPELL & Co., LTD.)
PRIN. VIOLIN - MR. MAURICE SONS
ORGANIST - MR. FREDK. B. KIDDLE

CONDUCTOR—
SIR HENRY J. WOOD.

SYMPHONY CONCERTS

BACH · HANDEL · SCHVBERT · BRAHMS · LISZT · WAGNER · BERLIOZ

BEETHOVEN · MOZART · HAYDN · MENDELSSOHN · SCHVMANN · WEBER · TCHAIKOVSKY

FRANK NVDD

ANALYTICAL PROGRAMME, ONE SHILLING.

The Concerts:

The First Thirty Years

"What was the usual Promenade Concert in those days? It was a halfway house between a symphony concert and the music hall."

© Hulton Deutsch Collection Ltd.

Caricature of Sir Thomas Beecham
© Hulton Deutsch Collection Ltd.

EMU.

'How many of my young Promenaders could stand and listen to it if I repeated it nowadays, I leave to their judgment. I doubt whether I could tolerate it myself, but both they and I must remember the conditions ruling then. This was a new venture and as such it had to be popular.'

So spoke Sir Henry Wood, many years later, of the first Promenade concert in the Queen's Hall which began at 8 p.m. on Saturday 10th August 1895. 'Stand' is the operative word, for many more than nowadays stood in the summer heat and poor ventilation of the concert hall where the decor, by explicit intention of the designer T.E. Knightley, was 'the colour of a London mouse's belly.' Smoking was permitted.

They would have needed stamina to endure the whole programme of twenty-five items which began with the National Anthem and Wagner's overture *Rienzi*. Really it was a concert of the sort which Sir Thomas Beecham used to describe as 'lollipops' - some of the lollipops sweeter than others. There were delights and excitements: Chopin's marvellous *Polonaise in A* and the gipsy fervour of Liszt's *Second Hungarian Rhapsody*, the 'Tra-la-la Figaro' which everyone knew, its real name *Largo al Factotum* from *The Barber of Seville*. That is the aria in which amateur singers used to try to outrace one another.

They played Schubert's lovely *Serenade,* but on a cornet! The cornet solo was a popular favourite in late Victorian and Edwardian times - a more sedate equivalent of that number in the modern rock concert when the lead guitarist smashes his instrument. Highlights from *Carmen*, Chabrier's *Habanera* - which surely had them swinging - and a few more old warhorses and there was a first night to remember.

The Queen's Hall was built to accommodate 2492 people and it was more than half-filled on 10th August 1895.

Sir Thomas Beecham

© Hulton Deutsch Collection Ltd.

What was the usual Promenade concert in those days? It was a halfway house between a symphony concert and the music hall, an alternative to the morbid portentousness of third rate oratorios, which were crinoline and old lace Victoriana, all sentimentality and diminished chords - original sin as it were, orchestrated with the utmost sugariness. A Promenade concert meant pop-classics: love songs, dashing overtures and bright military marches; and virtuoso solo performances on trumpet and bassoon which belonged as much in the circus as the concert hall.

What made the Wood Proms different was the quality of the orchestral playing and the determination of the conductor to put on first performances - 'novelties' as he called them - of works by living composers. Even in that very first concert Wood had included a novelty: the *Grand March* by Schloesser. Who today has heard of Schloesser?

The Queens Hall in 1890.

© Hulton Deutsch Collection Ltd.

The persona of the conductor himself was a 19th century innovation. Mozart and his contemporaries directed the orchestra discreetly from the keyboard or at the fiddle, but the idea of the conductor as demonic genius, all powerful wizard and sex-symbol is part of the gothic atmosphere of the romantic age. This was the era of the heavily-repressed sexuality of the Brontës' sodden and misty moorland; or Mary Shelley's *Frankenstein* and Bram Stoker's *Dracula*. There was more than a hint of Dracula about the hypnotic, Transylvanian Franz Liszt. Wood, by all accounts, was neither a mesmeric sex god nor over-extravagant in his gestures on the platform, but he too must have inherited some at least of the mystique of the conductor. His nickname was 'Timber' from the beginning.

Admission was 1/- (5p) into the Promenade or the Balcony while a place in the Grand Circle cost half a crown (12.5p) and season tickets - August to October - were a guinea (£1.05).

People came to hear an exciting tune so there was always plenty of Beethoven on the programme and thrilling brassy pieces by such as Rimskykorsakov. The bright, scintillating *A major symphony, The Italian,* by Mendelssohn was a favourite. Mendelssohn was ever popular. He had been a favourite of Queen Victoria herself. But, as well as a merry dance, the audiences loved a good cry and these were provided in plenty. Sullivan's maudlin ballad *The Lost Chord* played to a full house in the 1895 season, as it did in many years to come:

'Seated one day at the organ, I was weary and ill at ease

When my fingers wondered idly over the noisy keys...'

How could it fail? It had just the right combination of magic, wistfulness and dead leaves spirituality about it to define the last decade of Victorian England. All crocodile tears

and aspidistras. But in that first season Wood included compositions by members of his own orchestra.

Barnum and Bailey had nothing on Wood and Newman! To accompany the second season of concerts, Newman showed animated pictures in the interval for a charge of sixpence (2.5p). These bore such titles as *Up The River, Arrival of the Paris Express* and *Ladies Drilling* (!). They were precursors of the movies and wildly popular except with members of the orchestra who preferred to spend their intervals in The Glue Pot pub in Great Portland Street.

By 1896, Mondays were established as Wagner nights. To appreciate the novelty and daring of this programming you would have to imagine a popular, regular concert today of music from the 1960s and 1970s - that is of modern 'serious' music, not pop. It is hard to imagine that such as Ligeti, Boulez, Stockhausen and Elliott Carter would, if all put on the same programme, play to packed houses in any concert hall in Britain today.

But in 1896 Europe was besotted with Wagner, new as he was then. There is a very simple explanation for why, in those days, audiences took more readily to new music than they do today: it was either that or nothing. There was no gramophone. There was no radio. New music did not have to compete for a hearing with magnificent recordings of the best of the familiar classics played in a variety of styles by the world's finest orchestras - and all in the comfort of one's sitting room.

Monday night was Wagner night and Friday night was Beethoven night but in between you might hear anything, almost, from *Act Three* of Gounod's *Faust* to a medley from The Park Sisters. Not all the performances were of equal excellence. For example in that 1896 season one soprano got so lost in her singing that Wood had to leave the podium and go down and accompany her on the

piano - to a tumult of sympathetic applause. But the emphasis was Wagner, so much so that Wood said, 'Whether I was popularising Wagner or he was doing a like service for me was difficult to decide.' For all this, a member of the orchestra was paid forty-five shillings (£2.25) per week for six concerts and three rehearsals - and the concerts were not over usually until 11 p.m.

Another favourite was the overture to *William Tell* and this was first played at the Proms in 1897. The Promenaders loved Rossini's overtures - they still do - for their gradual acceleration to the point of mayhem and for the composer's mastery of the perpetual penultimate climax. They also shouted and cheered for Wagner's *The Ride of the Valkyries,* so clanging and boisterous that it sounds like old tramcars of control. Queen Victoria herself admired Wagner and she told Wood so when she attended a Prom in 1898 - but to hear the calmer, more reflective music of the sacred drama *Parsifal,* was more to her liking

There was a real novelty in 1898: Edward Elgar billed as 'one of the most promising of the younger generation of English composers.' He was forty-one at the time. And the following year

saw the appearance of one of the many child prodigies to enthrall the Promenade audiences over the years: the twelve year old Paul Bazelaire playing the new and extremely difficult *Cello Concerto* by Saint-Saens. Incidentally, Saint-Saens forbade performances of his delightful piece *The Carnival of the Animals* during his lifetime because he believed it to be unworthy of him, 'trivial.' The British public at that time did not really believe that our composers were as good as the continentals and yet this attitude combined with the performance of concerts to celebrate great national occasions. So in 1900 there was a 'Thanksgiving Concert to Celebrate the Victory of the Imperial Troops in South Africa.' And, from the majestic to the mildly surreal, there was the premier of *Three Blind Mice* by Josef Holbrooke (British).

There was a temporary setback in 1901 arising out of Robert Newman's increasing debts which accrued through his over-ambitious theatrical ventures. In the nich of time Sir Edgar Speyer, a German-born banker who had risen to become a Privy Counsellor, organised a syndicate to pay for all the orchestra'a financial needs. Speyer was an enthusiast for music and a man of wide culture. His happy association with the Queens's Hall Orchestra continued until 1915. The new lessees of the Queen's Hall were Chappell the publishers but they had no say in the choice of music.

In 1901 Wilhelm Backhaus played Mendelssohn's *G Minor Piano Concerto* and another great occasion was the appearance of Sibelius to hear Wood conduct the *King Christian Suite.* But the event of that year - the year overshadowed by Queen Victoria's death - was the first performance of Elgar's *Pomp and Circumstance March Number One.* 'The people simply rose and yelled,' wrote Wood. No one then knew that it would become 'the second National Anthem', *Land of Hope and Glory* or that it would one day be the tune by which the Proms are universally recognised.

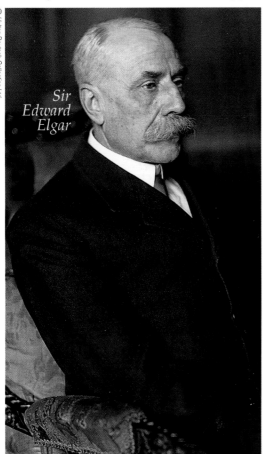

© Hulton Deutsch Collection Ltd

Sir
Edward
Elgar

Also in 1901 there was the occasion for a little bawdy hilarity when the announcer introduced the *Piano Concerto Opus 28* by Ludwig Schytte..

By 1902 the orchestra contained more than ninety pieces and the season was graced by a visit from King Edward and Queen Alexandra at a Sunday afternoon Prom. That season saw the first performance in England of Cesar Franck's *Symphonic Variations* for piano and orchestra - a piece which, because of the rhythm of its opening phrase, often repeated, is known to many orchestral musicians as 'Get your hair cut!' The great warhorses of 20th century music made many of their early appearances at the Queen's Hall. In 1903 Elgar's *Enigma Variations* provoked a near riot of emotional ecstasy, everyone trying to puzzle out the mysteries which lay behind each movement. Favourite of all the *Variations* is, of course, *Nimrod* named after Elgar's friend Jaeger and it has been conjectured that the mysterious theme with which *Nimrod* connects contrapuntally is the slow movement from Beethoven's piano sonata in C minor, the *Pathetique.* Others have paired it with a Mozart movement. Always the formula persisted: warhorses and novelties. They played everything from the lightest, frothiest piece of salon music, 'mere creations' as Wood said, to the most sublime creations of the modern masters. In 1904, for example, there appeared both music by ebullient young Australian pianist Percy Grainger and the masterpiece by Debussy, *Prelude A L'Apresmidi D'une Faune.* This is the piece which Pierre Boulez has said marks the beginning of 20th century music.

There was an amusing incident in 1904 - the Proms are celebrated for their amusing incidents! Donal Tovey was the soloist in *Book One* of Brahm's *Paganini Variations* which were so rapturously received that the soloist agreed to play 'a brief encore.' Whereupon he immediately sat down and played the whole of *Book Two* with the result that the rest of the concert had to be cancelled - run out of time!

The year before had seen the first performance in England of Mahler's *First Symphony*, that great and pioneering work of which Neville Cardus once said, 'This symphony is not at all as bad as it sounds.' It is a Promenade favourite now - everyone knows the mock-macabre setting in the third movement of *Frére Jacques* in a minor key - but how new it was in 1903. Bruckner's *Seventh* was played in the same season.

In 1904 Wood was offered the annual engagement of three months' concerts at New York's Carnegie Hall but he turned it down in order to give his best to the Proms. He returned from America to one of his greatest and most abiding successes: his arrangement of the *Fantasia on British Sea Songs* which was first performed on 21st October 1905 to mark the centenary of Nelson's victory at Trafalgar. Once in all the succeeding years was this piece left out of the programme but there was a commotion and it had to be restored for the very next season. It has, of course, become a ritual part of the Last Night, an occasion for cheerful pandemonium in the audience and orchestra alike. 'It is a race I like to win by two bars if possible,' said Wood.

One of the ways in which Wood improved orchestral playing in London was by his, and Newman's, abolishing the so-called deputy system which was the plague of all musical standards in the capital. It worked like this: an instrumentalist would go along to a rehearsal for which he would be paid; come the day of the concert he may have found an engagement which would pay him more than the concert for which he had practised. So he would send along his deputy to the rehearsed concert and he himself would play the second concert. In this way it often turned out that both concerts were played by men who had not actually practised the pieces on the programme.

Sir Edward
Elgar with
Beatrice
Harrison

The interior of The Queens Hall, 1894

Newman and Wood agreed that, for quality's sake, they would no longer tolerate the deputy system. It was done at a stroke. One day in 1904, Robert Newman mounted the platform and said, 'Gentlemen, there will be no deputies. Good morning!' Whereupon forty members resigned and formed the core of the London Symphony Orchestra which gave its first concert under the legendary Richter.

The quality of the Queen's Hall Orchestra gradually improved. In 1905 they gave the first British performance of Mahler's *Fourth Symphony*, a long romantic piece with an extended soprano solo *A Child's Vision of Heaven* which was sung by

Wood's wife, Olga. In the same year they played Sibelius' *Swan of Tuonela* with the composer present once again. They followed this with *Finlandia* in 1906.

A measure of the orchestra's talent and self-confidence can be seen in an incident from 1908. Debussy was conducting one of his own works and he lost his way in the middle of the piece.

A shy and diffident man, he was covered with embarrassment and he signalled to the orchestra to stop. But they would not. They had rehearsed the piece, they knew it well and they were very fond of it. They played it through to the

conclusion and received great applause - particularly from the composer himself!

The years immediately before the First World War saw an astonishing number of 'firsts' and triumphs which put the Promenade concerts at the centre of British musical life. In 1909 they gave Mahler's *Adagietto,* that movement from his *Fifth Symphony* which has become famous in our time as the theme music from Visconti's film of Mann's novel, *Death In Venice.* There was also a performance of Elgar's new *A Flat Symphony* and, in 1911, the first performance of the waltz from *Der Rosenkavalier* caused a sensation.

The first decade of the 20th century saw an enormous upheaval in the whole realm of human thought. These were the years of Einstein's Theory of Relativity and of Max Planck's elaboration of quantum mechanics. In art Picasso and Braque exhibited the first pictures in the Cubist style and in music Arnold Schoenberg was causing a scandal across Europe with his so-called 'atonal' works. Something, in the general cultural sense, was in the air. It was a revolutionary age.

There were many influences behind the new music, one of which was the feeling that the exceedingly long romantic pieces by the late 19th century's greatest composers - Wagner, Bruckner and Mahler - had stretched the harmonic tensions of the traditional system of musical keys to its limit. In 1908 Schoenberg deliberately ignored all previous notions of keys and of composing in keys - C major, B Flat minor or whatever. His new music was given a hostile welcome by audiences to the degree that in later years Schoenberg and his friends formed The Society for the Private Performance of Music.

In the face of this revolution in music, Wood showed that he was no reactionary, no mere provincial. He performed Schoenberg's *Five Orchestral Pieces* at the Queen's Hall in 1912 and he was hissed. He remarked afterwards, 'This, I

think, goes to refute the popular idea that the Promenaders accord acclamation to every work played, no matter what.'

The programme-note had said of *Five Orchestral Pieces:* 'They are merely experiments in dissonance; protests against all preconceived notions of music and harmony.' The point is that Wood played them, thus showing at once his own willingness to give all sorts of music a hearing and the versatile talent of his orchestra. Typical of the 'all sorts' nature of the Proms is that a season which played Schoenberg at his most cacophonous and intransigent also offered Elgar's new *Coronation March* and Percy Grainger's squib *Molly On The Shore.*

And in one superb season, 1913, besides the regular Wagner nights (Mondays) and Beethoven nights (Fridays) Wood played Stravinsky's *Firebird* suite - 'the music is not of the kind that lends itself to verbal analysis', said the programme; Vaughan Williams *The Wasps,* new works by Faure and Ravel as well as Debussy's *Iberia* and Mahler's *The Song of the Earth* - that very orchestration of the end of an era, of the long Edwardian twilight before the horrors of modernity in the form of the 1914-18 war.

In 1919 the Queen's Hall lost its 'mouse's belly' appearance and it was newly decorated bluish-green. The new leader of the orchestra, Charles Woodhouse, used to conduct for rehearsals sometimes and this enabled Wood to listen from the back of the hall. It was from there that he first made use of his bell to attract the orchestra's attention - sometimes to stop them in full flight - to their general annoyance. Wood was awarded the Gold Medal of the Royal Philharmonic Society in 1921, for services to music. Previous holders of the medal had included Brahms and Paderewski.

In 1921 Malcolm Sargent, aged twenty-six (just the age Wood had been when he first conducted

the Proms) conducted the Queen's Hall Orchestra in his own composition, *An Impression On A Windy Day*. The story has it that, a fortnight before the concert was due to be played, Wood enquired of the composer about the piece and he was alarmed to discover that it was not yet finished. Sargent replied to Wood's anxious questioning that he would complete it 'easy'. Wood was not pleased with Sargent's attitude. The piece was given on time and there was no lasting disagreement between the two men.

In the immediate postwar years the Wagner nights included much of what one critic referred to as 'great bleeding chunks of' *The Ring* - that great cycle of which it was once remarked, 'Wagner has some lovely moments but some terrible threequarters of an hour...' Modernity and pastiche sat side by side as, for instance, in perfor-mances of Prokofiev's *First Piano Concerto* and Landon Ronald's *The Garden of Allah*.

George V and Queen Mary attended a concert and Elgar, Master of the King's Music, conducted his *Cockaigne* overture. For cheerfulness and loud applause, this Prom was compared to a Cup Final.

Gustav Holst, sometime trombonist in the Queen's Hall Orchestra, conducted his new suite *The Planets* and there was a tumultuous reception for Elgar's new symphonic poem *Falstaff*. In 1922 there was more booing - this time of *Petrushka* by Stravinsky. Booing was only a small sort of disturbance: there had been riots and fires in Paris to greet *The Rite of Spring*.

When classical music is mentioned or, worse still, 'serious' music, some mouths turn down at the corners and faces crease in frowns. It was never meant to be like this. The great composers themselves were among the most

© The Lebrecht Collection

sparkling company anyone 'could wish to keep and the Promenade concerts were always intended to present music as something to lift the spirits. There are probably more jokes and more humorous situations involving musicians than any other profession with the possible exceptions of clergymen and undertakers. The Proms have always had more than their share of characters, for example Leon Goossens the wonderful oboist.

Goossens was once chided by Wood for 'buoyancy of spirits' - a euphemism for the oboist's habit of constant joke-telling, winking and passing round bits of paper while on the platform. He replied to Wood's censure in a most polite written message which utterly took the sting out of the situation: 'I am tremendously sorry for the worry and trouble I have caused you, and only wish I had been pulled up before.' It was typical of the man. And typical of Wood, too, that he should tell this story against himself. In 1922 Maggie Teyte sang *Tatiana's Letter Song* from *Eugene Onegin* and confessed that her real name was 'Tate' but she had changed it because the French tended to pronounce it 'Tart'. Jokes apart, Maggie Teyte probably knew more than anyone else about the new Impressionist music from France and it was she who helped popularise this style especially among the Promenaders. Saint-Saens died in 1921 and so his lifetime ban on *Carnival of the Animals* lapsed and it was given its first British performance in the 1923 season. Also in 1923, the soprano Isobel Baillie, 'the baker's girl' - her father had been a baker in Hawick - made her debut and remained in constant demand for the next fifty years. She sang in more than a thousand performances of *Messiah*. And it was the year of the first Proms performance of Elgar's *Cello Concerto* - by Beatrice Harrison.

Sir
Malcolm
Sargent

© Hulton Deutsch Collection Ltd.

The following year saw the repeat of *An Impression On A Windy Day* which provoked some ribaldry in the rehearsal. Sargent had already cultivated the dashing, debonair image - 'smile like a piano keyboard' - and a brass player was heard to call out (perhaps more loudly than he had intended), 'Look out - here come Sargent with the wind!'

'Novelties' introduced by Wood were not always pieces recently composed. There were in those days centuries of music scarcely heard including much from the glory days of English sacred music. This was at least partly remedied in 1925 when the tercentenary of Orlando Gibbons was celebrated. An examination of the programme for that year shows the range and depth of musical education and entertainment afforded by the Promenade concerts. Apart from Gibbon's glorious polyphony there were virtuoso performances by two of the greatest organists alive: Edward Bairstow and Harold Darke. There was Ibert's *Ballad of Reading Gaol* and an astonishing piece of mechanical futurism in Honegger's *Pacific 231* - impressions of a US railway engine. All these things neatly slotted in among what had become by this time staple fare: Bach, Beethoven, Brahms, Tchaikovsky and Wagner. The musical life of the nation had been enriched beyond measure in a mere thirty years.

1926 brought sadness in that it was the year of the death of the man who had done more than any other - except Wood himself - to bring music to the people. Robert Newman died, aged sixty-nine. There was a memorial concert, of course, and Wood played his own arrangement of Chopin's *Funeral March* on 6th November. W.W. Thompson, aged twenty-six, who had been Newman's assistant, took over and Wood wrote that he 'managed the orchestra with assurance, tact and ability.'

The Promenade concerts were Newman's baby and he had lived to see the baby not only alive and kicking but increasing in maturity and stature with every year.

The War Years

"The war can't last three months
and the public will need its music
and, incidentally, our orchestra
its salaries."

© Hulton Deutsch Collection Ltd.

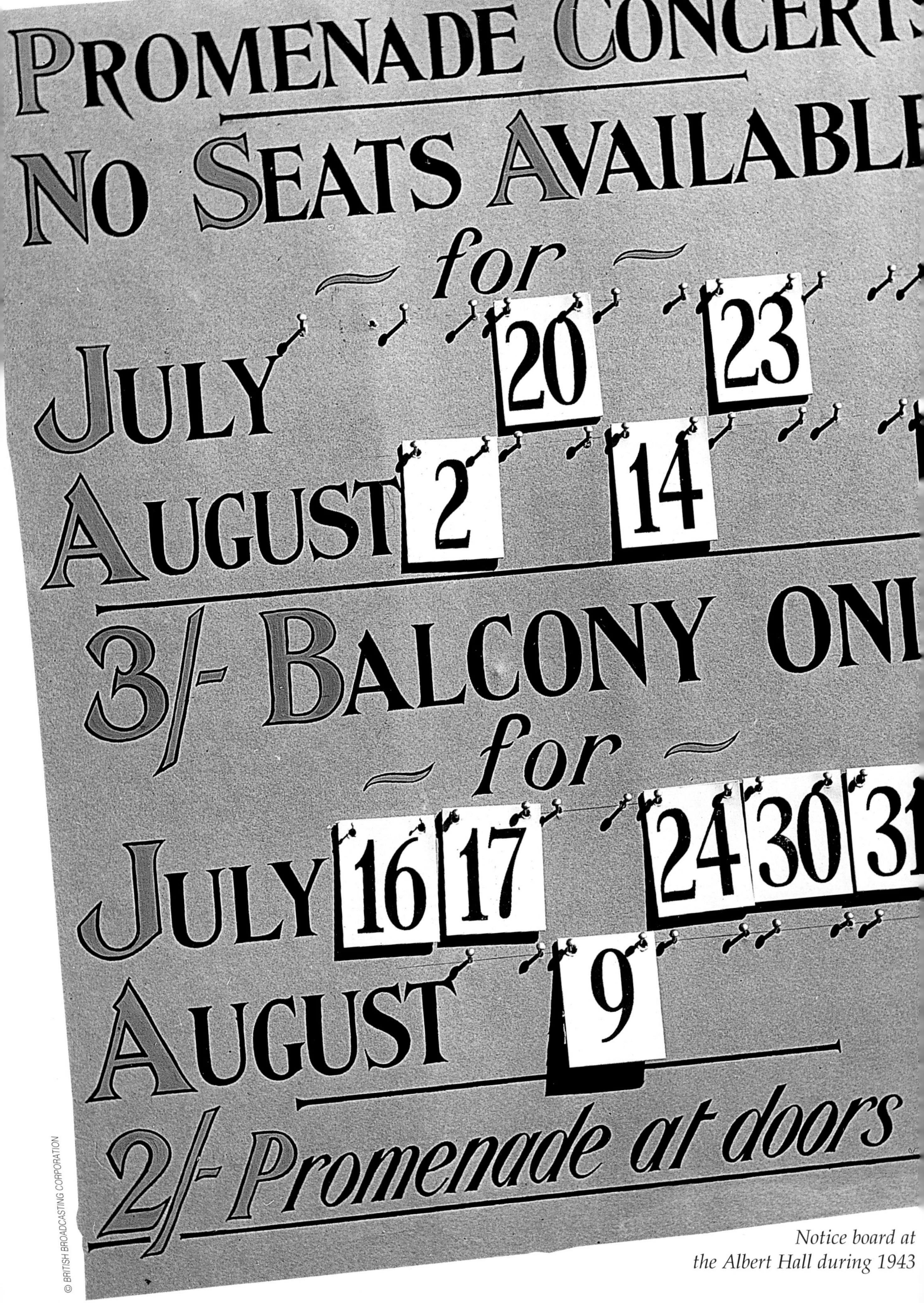

PROMENADE CONCERTS

NO SEATS AVAILABLE
~ for ~

JULY   20   23

AUGUST   2   14

3/- BALCONY ONLY
~ for ~

JULY   16 17   24 30 31

AUGUST   9

2/- Promenade at doors

© BRITISH BROADCASTING CORPORATION

*Notice board at
the Albert Hall during 1943*

The long, dreamy twilight of European romanticism was shattered on 4th August 1914 when the nations went to war and all the dark and violent prophecies of modern artistic movements - Expressionism, Cubism, new poetry and atonalism in music - seemed to come true at a stroke.

Should the Proms continue? Robert Newman had no doubt: 'Why not?' he said 'The war can't last three months and the public will need its music and, incidentally, our orchestra its salaries.' And so the Proms did go ahead but not without some difficulties.

Sir Edgar Speyer who since Newman's financial difficulties of 1901, had probably backed the Promenade concerts with about £30,000 of his own money, was insulted verbally and in the press on account of his German origins. Anti-German feeling had been whipped up by the authorities - it was the period when stories about the bayoneting of babies by German soldiers were in wide circulation - and Sir Edgar's position became intolerable. He wrote to the Prime Minister, Asquith, and resigned his Privy Counsellorship but Asquith, to his great credit, refused to accept the resignation. Still, Speyer felt he could not continue and he withdrew to America.

In the Queen's Hall itself there was trouble and rowdyism on the Monday Wagner night and on 17th August the Wagner concert was replaced with one which included works by British, French and Russian composers - the so-called 'music of the Allies'. This concert began with the National Anthem and ended with La Marseillaise.

Newman was asked in letters to ban all German music from the Proms. Courageously Newman replied in the programme: 'We take this opportunity of emphatically contradicting the statements that German music will be boycotted

during the present season. The greatest examples of Music and Art are world possessions and unassailable even by the prejudices and passions of the hour.'

Wagner was then reinstated and played on Monday nights for the duration.

A bronze bust of King George V was positioned in the Queen's Hall and flags of the Allies were perpetually displayed in a prominent position. The Allies' national anthems were arranged by Wood and played over and over - as he confessed - to his 'untold boredom.'

After Speyer's departure, Chappells became responsible for managing the orchestra which was now known as The New Queen's Hall Orchestra. Audiences were depleted and there were losses, but these were offset to some extent by publicity for Chappell pianos and sheet music which the Proms advertised. There were hardly any foreign soloists at the concerts and this was only to be expected as 'the North Sea was no playground.' Many British players had left the orchestra to join the army or the navy.

Despite all, the concerts continued nightly. Zeppelin raids held back audiences until long after the performances had finished but they organised sing-songs and musical quizzes, talent competitions and other forms of musical do-it-yourself. In 1915 Wood continued to conduct with plaster falling around him and a soloist, to tremendous laughter, sang an encore: We Won't Go Home 'Til Morning!

The 1915 season was successful and three extra matinees were put on, making sixty-six concerts in all.

One significant advance encouraged by the emergency was the presence of more women in the orchestra. Beecham had opposed lady musicians in his bands for, as he said, 'If they're

Queens Hall showing bomb damage in the Second World War.

© Hulton Deutsch Collection Ltd.

pretty, they distract the other players; if they're ugly, they distract me.' Wood knew no such chauvinism. It was during the war that Wood received the offer of a post from the Boston Symphony Orchestra which would have involved his playing in the US for six months in the year. He was deluged with 'Stay at home Sir Henry!' letters and he declined the American offer. This was at great personal cost, for it meant giving up the opportunity to direct one of the world's most prestigious orchestras and America itself must have seemed a safe haven by comparison with our own embattled islands.

Wood's decision very probably saved the Promenade Concerts. Astonishingly the quality of the music held up even in wartime. In 1914 alone there were debuts of two of the world's greatest pianists: Moiseiwitsch, and Solomon aged eleven. Wood recalled, 'Solomon appealed tremendously to the audience with his winning, soulful eyes, his little silk shirt and short knickers.' In that same year there was a minor rebellion by some of the players who took against what they regarded as the 'strange and cacophonous' music in a new suite for orchestra by Bela Bartok.

There were new delights even in the Great War. Mussorgsky's powerful *Pictures From An Exhibition* was given a first performance and so was Ethel Smyth's *The Boatswain's Mate.* The lady composer was a prominent feminist and she had colourful methods of complaining that men had stolen music for themselves and wished to keep it well out of women's influence: 'One afternoon while Adam was asleep, Eve, anticipating the Great God Pan, bored some holes in a hollow reed and began to do what is called "pick out a tune". Thereupon Adam spoke: "Stop that horrible noise," he roared, adding, "besides which, if anyone's going to make it, it's not you but me!"'

In 1916 there were performed two works which have remained favourites ever since: Rimsky Korsakov's *Scheherazade* and *Espana* by

Chabrier. The following year there was a moving performance of George Butterworth's *A Shropshire Lad.* Butterworth had been killed in action, aged twenty-one, in 1916. 1918 saw two pieces which in their separate ways can only be described as 'completely different.' The first was *Adventures in a Perambulator* by the American John Alden Carpenter and the second was *The Divine Poem* by Scriabin.

Scriabin was, to be gentle about it, 'unusual.' He was a self-proclaimed mystical philosopher and a compulsive hand-washer. He was forever in front of the mirror or worrying about his baldness, or worrying about his hypochondria! He came to believe that he was in control of the whole world. 'I am God! I am nothing. I am play. I am freedom. I am life. I am the boundary! I am the peak!' No bland rations for the Promenaders then, even in wartime!

The Second World War caused much greater disruption to the Proms than the First War had done, and it almost brought about the end of the concerts altogether. There had been enormous foreboding since the Munich agreement in 1938 which many people had understood only as an opportunity to buy time. The fleet was mobilised. On Friday 1st September 1939 the concert was curtailed after Beethoven's *Pastoral Symphony* and Wood addressed the audience:

'Owing to the special arrangements for broadcasting which are now in force, the BBC very much regrets that the Symphony Orchestra will no longer be available for these concerts in London. I am therefore very sorry to say that from tonight the Promenade Concerts will close down until further notice. I must thank you, my dear friends, for your loyal support, and I hope we shall soon meet again.' Beneath his calm exterior, Wood was raging. He thought that the Proms should have continued just as they had done between 1914-18, but the war restrictions this time were severe. All broadcasting was on one channel and this meant that music's share of total output was greatly reduced. The BBC took the Symphony Orchestra off to Bristol which was considered to be a safer location than London.

The BBC had taken over the running of the Proms in 1927 and this brought many blessings but it also brought interminable wrangling and ubiquitous committees. Wood detested this whole aspect. He became very depressed.

At last it was decided to hold a short season of concerts from 10th August 1940 until 7th September. The Queen's Hall was fitted out with air raid signs and the concerts continued uninterrupted. Wood, typically, lodged at the Langham Hotel, right next door in Portland Place and in the very centre of the most dangerous area. He remained there throughout the Blitz.

The First World War practice of remaining behind long after concerts had ended, waiting for the All Clear, was renewed and improved on so that it became something of a regular party. Basil Cameron, Wood's Associate Conductor, organised music quizzes and Gerald Moore would accompany from memory or by improvisation all requests for songs. There were talent competitions for members of the audience - competitions which became almost as popular as the concerts themselves. The last Promenade concert to be played in the Queen's Hall was on 7th September 1940 and one of the last pieces to be played was Holbrooke's *Three Blind Mice*.

But it was not the last concert of all to be played there. That was not a Prom, but a performance of Elgar's *Dream of Gerontius* directed by Malcolm Sargent on 10th May 1941. Shortly afterwards the Ministry of Information announced:

'For five moonlit hours, over three hundred bombers dropped great numbers of incendiaries and high explosives, causing a serious fire situation, setting a new record for casualty figures (1436 killed and 1792 injured) and doing great damage to public buildings. The House of Commons Chamber was destroyed. Westminster Abbey was hit; so were the British Museum, the Law Courts, the War Office, the Mint, the Mansion House and the Tower. Five of the Halls of the City Companies were destroyed and many famous churches were damaged.'

The Queen's Hall was gutted and there was little the firemen, hampered by burst water-mains, could do to retrieve it. But the bronze bust of Wood in the auditorium was undamaged and

eutsch Collection Ltd.

to this day it is carried each year to the Royal Albert Hall by two Promenaders where it is crowned with a laurel wreath.

David Cox managed to discover one piece of glad tidings in the debacle: 'The German bomb wiped out (besides much else) the history of difficult relations between Chappell's and the BBC' and in 1941 the Proms were held in the Royal Albert Hall.

The RAH, opened in 1871, is twice the size of the Queen's Hall and this caused severe acoustical problems. It could accommodate 1250 standing, 1150 in the gallery and 4900 seated but its vastness could be the ruin of a musical performance. As George Bernard Shaw remarked, 'The Albert Hall is the best musical bargain in town. Pay once and you can hear the music twice!' Such were the difficulties caused by its infamous echo.

Experts from the Government Building Research Station at Hope Bagenal were consulted and it was decided to provide orchestra screens, a chained roof and a flat surface resonator to be placed behind the conductor. In addition the ventilation was legendarily awful - and it still is!

To venture out in the evenings in London during the War was to court death and so, for a time at least, audiences were smaller than they had been in better times and at the Queen's Hall. Wood wrote, 'I was obliged to avoid novelties and other musical satisfactions, for as everyone knows, to close down meant defeat and disaster from which even my courage and renown might never recover.' It was in 1941 that Wood, aged seventy-two, agreed to share the burden of conducting with his Associate, Basil Cameron. Adversity bred spirit however and Wood recalled 1942 as 'a glorious season.'

It was also the year which inaugurated the institution of the Last Night Speech. Wood addressed them affectionately: 'I must thank you and tell you what a wonderful audience you have been. How you listen! Your attention is so encouraging and exhilarating.'

And, through the medium of radio, the positive effects of the concerts reached the whole nation. 'People ask what is going on,' said Churchill. 'The answer is, We are going on.' The Proms were, like the Nine O'Clock News, like the speeches of the Prime Minister, a sign that the nation was undefeated. The musicians themselves were aware of their important role and this helped them tremendously to maintain their enthusiasm and dedication.

As in World War I, there were few foreign soloists and many experienced orchestral players had left to join the armed forces. Even so, a very high standard of musicianship and repertoire was maintained for the duration. Once again 'music of the Allies' was featured, most spectacularly in Shostakovich's *Leningrad Symphony* which captured the public's imagination with its portrayal of the siege of that great city. Less successful was the performance of the *Symphony in C* by the communist Alan Bush. Russia was our ally and there were a few examples of 'hands across the sea' gestures of this sort, but the Bush symphony was not well received and there was something of a rumpus.

1942 also saw the first performance of Benjamin Britten's *Sinfonia da Requiem*. Of course *Beethoven's Fifth* was a favourite, not least because the rhythm of its opening notes was used as the famous 'Victory' call sign in the Morse Code - di, di, di, dah. Our American allies were celebrated also in the first Proms performance of Aaron Copland's ballet suite *Billy the Kid*. Earlier Wood had conducted Lennox Berkeley's *Introduction And Allegro For Two Pianos And Orchestra* and described it as 'modern *but* good!' He also offered the *Three Pieces For Orchestra* by Elizabeth Lutyens and he was glad when it was received without acclaim. 'Thank God,' said Wood' - only five

minutes of excessive boredom!' Joseph Kennedy, father of John and American Ambassador, attended many of the wartime Proms.

1944 saw appearances by two hugely popular pianists, Eileen Joyce and Myra Hess who became as much part of wartime cultural mythology as Glen Miller and Vera Lynn. It was also - flying bombs and all - the fiftieth season of the Promenade concerts and of the Jubilee concert which, alas, found Wood absent in the throes of his final illness.

© BRITISH BROADCASTING CORPORATION

The Involvement of the BBC

"There is no doubt that the wireless will inherit the earth, for it is an invention as potent as the printing press. No aspect of life will remain unaltered by it. It will spell the end of the music hall."

© BRITISH BROADCASTING CORPORATION

By the middle of the 1920s the BBC had established the century's great revolution in public entertainment. It was an unprecedented and almost unimaginable change and the social and cultural prognostications were various, D.B. Carteris' words in *The Spectator* being typical: 'There is no doubt that the wireless will inherit the earth for it is an invention as potent as the printing press, as fundamental to our common life as our common language. It will be soon in every home and it will gather refinements. No aspect of life will remain unaltered by it. It will spell the end of the music hall.'

How fascinating that such a farsighted piece of prophecy bordering on the apocalyptic should conclude with the end of the music hall as the most disastrous consequence! It was the end of the music hall but the start of so much else. Many people in the rest of the entertainment industry claimed that the BBC enjoyed an unfair advantage. William Boosey, Managing Director of Chappells who were sponsoring the Proms, said, 'The BBC is a competitor of the entertainment industry, paying no entertainment tax but being absolutely subsidised by the government.' And on 7th March 1927 Chappells announced that they could no longer support the Proms.

Wood at once made a statement to the press: 'It would be a disgrace to this country if the Proms were to go. It would give continentals an opportunity to call us unmusical.'

The BBC had been awarded its charter in 1927 'to inform, educate and entertain' and its Director General John Reith said that this involved the Corporation in the duty 'to promote the highest interests of the community and of the nation at large.' Percy Pitt, the BBC's Director of Music saw one of the highest interests as the provision of concerts of high quality and popular appeal and he wanted to take over the Proms. William Boosey, who already regarded the wireless as a threat to his company's sales of pianos and sheet music, objected to the plan. But when the BBC countered with its own scheme to run a new series of Proms at the Central Hall, Boosey backed down and an agreement was struck which involved him, the BBC and the Musicians' Union.

The Promenade Concerts began their first season of BBC sponsorship on 13th August 1927. The BBC did not come raw to the experience for, even before it sponsored the Proms, two thirds of its whole output was music. The Corporation ran the permanent Welsh Orchestra and put on joint productions with such as the Hallé Orchestra and the British National Opera Company. There were many live symphony concerts, a weekly programme of chamber music and relays from Covent Garden and the provincial opera houses. Already in 1927 there had been the great success of the broadcast concert for Elgar's seventieth birthday. Many sacred works and church services were relayed by the BBC and in addition to all these attractions there was a huge popular audience for military band music and for dance bands.

From the beginning Eric Blom supervised the writing of the programme notes for the Promenade concerts and these have now become collectors' items like the *Wisden* cricketers' almanac. Also from the very beginning, BBC involvement improved the quality of the concerts as, for example, the second part was upgraded to include more serious 'quality' songs. The result of all the changes was the exact opposite of what William Boosey had feared: broadcasting saved the Proms from almost certain extinction and in a very short time made them more popular than ever. Wood was delighted and, perhaps for the first time in the thirty-two years of the Proms' existence he felt that they were secure:

'With the wholehearted support of the wonderful medium of broadcasting,' he said at the time 'I feel I am at last on the threshold of realising my lifelong ambition of truly

democratising the message of music and making its beneficent effect universal.'

1927 began a change in the ethos of the Proms which continues to this day and this is defined by the revolution in the apparatus of management. During their first thirty years, the Promenade concerts were run by two or three individuals, a handful at the most. After 1927 they became subject to the bureaucratic control of the BBC with its committees, labyrinthine structures and power struggles. This was a whole world away from the morning when Newman had, on his own account, simply and brusquely announced, 'Gentlemen, there will be no more deputies.' From 1927 every decision made, each new policy established, was the result of a wrangle and the first such wrangle was over the orchestra's name. For three years the concerts were billed as given by 'Sir Henry Wood and his Symphony Orchestra.' In 1930 this band was merged with The London Wireless Orchestra and named The BBC Symphony Orchestra. Not least among the improvements brought in by the Corporation was the doubling of rehearsal time: rehearsals were now daily. Wood said he felt, 'free from the everlasting programme-versus-box-office problem for the first time in thirty-two years.'

Robert Newman's successor W.W. 'Tommy' Thompson stayed on as manager and he was soon appointed BBC Concerts Manager. The leader of the new orchestra - which numbered a hundred and fourteen players - was Charles Woodhouse and he was followed by Arthur Catterall. The BBC stated that its aim was to maintain one of the world's best orchestras. The broadcasts were hugely popular while at the same time live audiences increased and the standard ticket price was kept at two shillings (10p).

Musical highlights in those early days included Myra Hess' appearances in 1928 to play Bach, when Wood said he could have filled the Queen's Hall twice over. And in 1929 each

Thursday concert was given over to a programme featuring British composers and including such masterpieces as William Walton's *Viola Concerto* - with Hindemith playing the solo part, Peter Warlock's *Capriol Suite* and Lord Berners' *The Triumph of Neptune* which incidentally, was rapturously received when it was revived for the 1975 season.

Wood himself played a cheeky trick in 1929 which landed him in some controversy. He arranged an orchestral version of Bach's organ *Toccata and Fugue in D minor* and, knowing the British public's fondness for foreign names, claimed that the arrangement had actually been made by a one-time pupil of Glazunov called Klenovsky. Wood invented a 'biographical note' about 'Klenovsky' and had it put on the Proms Programme. *The Times* accused Wood of playing a poor joke on the public but Wood recorded 'enormous satisfaction' at the success of the spoof.

The extrovert conductor and self-publicist Leopold Stokowsky - who was actually born in the East End and died in Nether Wallop - had already produced an arrangement of Bach's *Toccata and Fugue* which later became very popular after its inclusion in Walt Disney's film *Fantasia*. At least part of Wood's motive in making his own arrangement was to outdo Stokowski and his version which Wood considered to be too much organ-centred for an orchestral piece.

In the 1931 season Poulenc played his *Aubade* and there was a performance of Elgar's *Nursery Suite* written in honour of the young princesses, Elizabeth and Margaret. There was a great rage at the time for Constant Lambert, who received the sort of accolade usually reserved for pop stars today, and his *Rio Grande* earned tumultuous applause. But in the same series much new and demanding music was played including 'twelve tone' works by Alban Berg and Anton Webern of the Second Viennese school as well as the delightful impressionistic *Gymnopedies* of

Erik Satie - still a great favourite, especially since it has featured in a television commercial.

The BBC did not 'play safe' in its programming but appointed Edward Clark, who had studied with Arnold Schoenberg, as Principal Programme Builder. Clark was a champion of new music and he included works by the British avant garde: Bax, Britten, Rubbra and Michael Tippett.

The 1930s saw a powerful strengthening of the Promenade concerts both musically and as a national institution. Wood was, of course, venerable by this time and praised wherever he appeared and he was superbly partnered by the BBCs new Director of Music, Adrian Boult who had already impressed with the Birmingham Symphony Orchestra. Paul Beard became leader in 1936, a position he held until 1962.

© Hulton Deutsch Collection Ltd.

Wagner was as popular as ever and in 1932 whole scenes from *The Ring* were played and a novelty of the season was Ravel's *Piano Concerto For Left Hand*, composed for Paul Wittgenstein (brother to the philosopher, Ludwig) who had lost an arm in the First World War. The centrepiece of 1933 was Elgar's *Second Symphony* and Neville Cardus wrote: 'Richard Strauss took off his hat to Elgar's music and that was enough for us; we could at last look the world in the face...' England was no longer, if it ever had been, 'the land without music.' For the great variety of music of a consistently high standard which was enjoyed in the 1930s and after, this country has the BBC to thank and chiefly for the Corporation's assiduous support of the Proms - even to the redecoration of the Queen's Hall in 1937 and the renewing of the lighting and ventilation systems.

The nation crept uneasily through the depression to the unleashing of a new and even more terrible war. There were milestones: the memorial concert for Elgar in 1934, Shostakovich's *First Symphony* and the *Fourth Symphony* of Vaughan Williams (1937) interpreted by Boult as a prophecy of the coming conflict. There were lighter moments as when for instance, at a performance of *Judas Maccabaeus*, Wood cut short the aria *Sound An Alarm* and a heckler called out from the auditorium, 'First you mutilate Wagner, and now you hack Handel!'

In 1938 Benjamin Britten was the soloist in his own *Piano Concerto* and, in that year, there was a twenty minute ovation for Wood on the Last Night. The 1939 season lasted for only three weeks, though it included an appearance by one of the greatest tenors of all time, Richard Tauber.

The first season after the war, 1945, was much less adventurous than most of those of the 1930s - all the novelties were put in the second halves of concerts and not broadcast. Thus two twentieth century masterpieces were denied an early hearing by a mass audience: Schoenberg's *Piano Concerto* and the *Four Sea Interludes* from Britten's new and disturbing opera, *Peter Grimes*.

The new Director of Music was Hely-Hutchinson who wrote to established composers, asking them to submit any works which they might have ready. The mood was conservative. Adrian Boult and Basil Cameron shared the conducting. The Monday Wagner night was done away with and the tradition for having Beethoven's *Ninth Symphony* on the penultimate night was established. Peter Pears made his debut singing in Britten's *Les Illuminations*.

It was the age of austerity with half of Europe in ruins and much of its population more than half starved. There were food shortages and

power cuts and the winter of 1947 was Arctic in its intensity - legendarily so. The country needed a spectacle such as a royal wedding to bring some cheerful relief and in November Princess Elizabeth, aged twenty-two, married Philip Mountbatten. The following November saw a Promenade concert of *Music For A Prince*, a suite by Jacob, Howells and Tippett to mark the birth of Prince Charles. In the same year the tradition of holding a short season of winter Proms was revived and this continued until 1952. Tickets for the first and last nights were allocated by ballot and there were twice as many applicants as seats available.

The immediate post war period was notable for the beginning of the ascendancy of Malcolm Sargent who had been appointed Associate Conductor in 1947, aged fifty-two. Sargent was stylish and debonair with the nickname 'Flash Harry' - probably invented by Beecham and well-known among all orchestral musicians. He was seen as an ambassador for music, a man of personality, wit and intelligence who might become a worthy successor to Wood.

In 1948 the BBC's new Director of Music was Steuart Wilson, a singer, but he did not hold the post for long and he was replaced by Herbert Murrill. Adrian Boult resigned, as he said, to concentrate on composing and so the conducting was shared between Sargent and Cameron. Three orchestras were used: the BBC Symphony Orchestra, the London Symphony and the London Philharmonic. Every note played at the Proms was broadcast by the Home Service, the Light Programme or the new and greatly admired Third Programme.

The conservatism of the period was accompanied by a big increase in the amount of

bureaucracy as what had been, literally, a one-man-band under Wood, now became a vast project involving dozens of people for six months every year to produce the programme. And then there was the problem of Sargent's personality.

He was hugely popular among audiences as a sort of proto-pop star but he upset orchestral musicians by his high-handedness in, for example, his demand that the BBC Symphony Orchestra should all stand when he entered the auditorium. They always refused. They disliked him for his glamour-boy attitude and in any case they knew that he had been only third choice for the job after Barbirolli and Kubelik. Sargent's efforts at self-aggrandisement failed in at least one other respect when the BBC turned down his request that the concerts be called the Wood-Sargent Proms.

To make matters worse, Sargent also had a cavalier attitude towards the music and one of his worst offences, amounting, as a critic at the time said, to an act of philistinism, was to cut Schubert's *Ninth Symphony* the 'Great' C Major: 'like cutting the third act of *Hamlet* or the *Coronation Oath*,' said Hugh Mallenson. Moreover, Sargent was very conventional, middle-brow, in his musical tastes and he disliked a great deal of twentieth century music and almost anything written after 1930. So the Proms lost much of the driving modernity and freshness which Wood had always provided.

Some went further. Maurice Johnstone, Head of Music (Sound) at the BBC said, 'Music is merely Sargent's shop-window. He has no sense of public, artistic or functional responsibility. He is indifferent to the morale and welfare of the orchestra. His sense of loyalty is non-existent.'

Johnstone hated the excessive frivolity which he detected at concerts and which he believed was ruining the tradition inherited from Wood. It was not simply that Edgar Mays had become famous

© Hulton Deutsch Collection Ltd

for raising and lowering the piano lid to the audience's encouragement, 'Heave!' but that a general rowdiness was threatening to take over the concerts, emasculate them as musical events and turn them instead into fashionable outings for Hooray Henrys - and Henriettas. He told Sargent: 'Some attempt must be made to curb the increasing hysteria of the audience and the only way that I can see is to present a much less frivolous type of programme.'

Sargent, perceiving the youngsters with their whistles and balloons, shouted out one night, 'Give the toys back to nanny!' The phrase itself says much about Sargent's own social milieu and his vision of whom the concerts were meant for. Johnstone struck a blow for sobriety by omitting Wood's *Fantasia On British Sea Songs* which he described as, 'badly constructed, merely a selection, unworthy, jingoism ...' The Promenaders protested with shouts and banners with the result that Johnstone allowed the *Sea Songs* as an encore and restored them fully to the programme for the following year, 1954.

Sargent was undeterred, knowing well the power of his public. He said, 'If people can get as enthusiastic about music as they do about football, then that is all to the good.' The First Night of the Proms was televised in 1953, Coronation Year and the Last Night in 1954. As Robert Simpson, the distinguished British composer remarked, 'The Proms now have an audience one seventh the size of Islam.'

How justified is the charge of conservatism over this period? Certainly there was a lack of adventurousness sometimes but this should not be exaggerated. For example, Walton's *Belshazzar's Feast* was performed in 1949 in the same season as Bartok's *Concerto for Orchestra* followed in 1950 by the same composer's *Viola Concerto* and Arnold Bax's *Concertante for Orchestra and Piano Left Hand*, written for Harriet Cohen who

had sprained her right wrist. 1952 heard Britten's *Viola Concerto* and the demanding *Sinfonietta* by Janacek was played to mark that composer's centenary in 1954. And there was Vaughan Williams' new *Sinfonia Antartica*.

An all Bach programme filled the hall in 1955 and in the same year Alban Berg's 'twelvetone' *Violin Concerto* was played - conducted not by Sargent but by Boult. More typical of the era was Sargent's introduction of Gilbert and Sullivan evenings.

The remaining years of the 1950s were largely taken up with the celebration of centenaries and memorials on the grand scale. 1956 was the two-hundredth anniversary of Mozart's birth and 1957 was Elgar's centenary for which his *The Dream of Gerontius* was given its first Proms performance. 1958 was Puccini's centenary which was marked by a whole act of *Tosca* and it was also the centenary of the founder Robert Newman and the orchestra played his great favourite *Softly Awakes My Heart* from *Samson and Delilah* by Saint-Saens. Haydn's *The Creation* was given its first Proms performance and so was Carl Orff's pseudo-medieval fantasy *Carmina Burana*.

In 1959 all nine Vaughan Williams symphonies were given in memory of the composer who had died the previous year. Tippett's *Ritual Dances* from *A Midsummer Marriage* were also performed. In that year William Glock was appointed Controller, Music at the BBC and this appointment marks the beginning of the modern age of the Promenade concerts.

Glock was a radical who had organised musical summer schools at the 'progressive' Dartington School in Devon and he operated with the slogan, 'It is our duty to be unpopular and popular at the same time.' He

diversified, increasing the number of conductors and orchestras to meet the demands of the specialities they were being asked to play. He also introduced young conductors and new, young soloists. Audiences fell by ten per cent in Glock's first two years in charge, 1960-61.

He had played Berio's *Perspectives*, so called 'electronic stuff' and Schoenberg's *Variations Opus 31* as well as such modern classics as Oedipus Rex by Stravinsky. In 1961 there were no fewer than fifty-six works new to the Proms. Yet, unbelievably in 1960, Mozart's great C Major *Piano Concerto K.503* had never been played at a Promenade concert, neither had Beethoven's *Missa Solemnis.* Glock introduced them both. Who could now believe that Mozart's *Requiem* had never been played at a Prom? But it had not until Glock put it on the programme in 1961.

It is fair to say that the creative cultural vitality returned to the Proms under Glock and, once he had learned the trick of pairing modern works with classical 'warhorses', audiences recovered and increased. The attractiveness of the broadcast concerts was greatly enhanced by the abolition of the Home Service's Nine O'Clock News. Incredibly, symphonies had been rudely cut short before this event. In 1962 there were sixty works new to the Proms and ten concerts were televised on BBC with a total audience of fifty million.

The range, scale and ambition of the concerts were increased enormously. Whole operas were performed including *Don Giovanni* and *Cosi Van Tutte*. Colin Davis conducted an eightieth birthday concert for Stravinsky and the astonishing *Oiseaux Exotiques* by Messiaen was performed, as well as Schoenberg's *Violin Concerto* and the young Peter Maxwell-Davies' *Fantasia On An In Nomine of John Taverner*. We speak of Schoenberg's music still as 'new' and 'modern' when perhaps we should recall that his composing career began in the 1890s. As Glock realised, it is the old problem: people will not

make the effort to listen to new music when what is old and well-known is played constantly on stereo systems of ever-increasing technological brilliance. Audiences need to have the new works constantly before them if living composers and the music of our own age are to become familiar.

Glock was Educator-in-Chief to the bourgoisie and his success was astounding. He introduced foreign orchestras and the tradition of Friday as the big First Night always featuring a single major work. He put on late night concerts in Chalk Farm in an old railway shed converted to be 'The Round House.' There was also regular visits to Covent Garden and Westminster Cathedral. Glock was a leading exponent of the performance of 'early' - that is to say pre-classical - music and in 1963 he put on Monteverdi's opera *Incoronazione di Poppea* and in 1971 Purcell's *The Fairy Queen,* conducted by Benjamin Britten. These were followed by another Monteverdi

© BRITISH BROADCASTING CORPORATION

masterpiece, *Il Ritorno d'Ulisse in Patria* conducted by Raymond Leppard with Janet Baker and Richard Lewis as principals.

Some said that Glock 'like all revolutionaries goes too far' and indeed his leadership of the Promenade concerts was not without controversy as when, for example, he scrapped *Pomp and Circumstance No. 1* in 1969 and thereby generated a public uproar. It was reinstated in 1970. Also the appointment of the 'dangerously avant garde' Pierre Boulez as the new Chief Conductor of the BBC Symphony Orchestra in 1971 raised hackles as well as eyebrows.

Glock was knighted in 1971 and he retired in 1972. In the meantime there had been a concert for the centenary of Henry Wood and Sargent had died (1967). Sir William Glock had not succeeded in turning the Proms into a forum for everything that was modern, if indeed that had ever been his entire aim. But his thirteen years in charge guaranteed that the Promenade concerts did not lapse and become an antiquarian phenomenon, an example of 'museum culture'. He preserved the classics while introducing an immense amount and variety of music to the unprecedented enrichment of the musical public.

There were glories, ancient and modern as Glock presented music from six hundred years of European tradition from plainsong and early opera to Varese and Stockhausen's *Kontakte*, the latter provoking a recollection of Sir Thomas Beecham who was once asked whether he had ever conducted any Stockhausen:
'No - but I think I once trod in some!'

In 1969 a performance of Maxwell Davies' *Worldes Blis* had required a piano turned on to its side and a collection of old metal tubes and an anvil. This was greeted with boos and desertions

© BRITISH BROADCASTING CORPORATION

*Richard Baker
presents the
Last Night
Broadcast.*

from the auditorium which demonstrates the fact that the Promenade audience was not an agglomeration of uncritical trendies any more than it had been a collection of musical reactionaries and mere nostalgics. There was jazz in 1971 in the form of George Newson's *Arena* with Cleo Lane and Jane Manning accompanied by film projections and flashing lights - 'not music for listening to,' as someone said at the time.

Extracts from the programmes for Glock's last season, 1973, in fact reveal the man's comprehensive vision. That series included the *Fourth* and *Fifth* symphonies of Beethoven - played by Karajan with the Berlin Philharmonic Orchestra to mark our entry into the Common Market - but also Robin Holloway's new *Evening With Angels* and Schoenberg's *Gurrelieder* and a long delayed revival of *Gloriana* by Benjamin Britten. Add to these attractions music for the Rachmaninov centenary and a seventieth birthday concert for Lennox Berkeley and it is impossible to accuse Glock of a narrow outlook in his pursuit of modernity.

In fact in the period of Glock's tenure the Proms developed both as an example of artistic excellence and as a spectacle and an annual party - this last aspect owing more and more to the increasing involvement of television. The concerts now sustained an audience whose size and range Wood could hardly have imagined.

Glock's successor was Robert Ponsonby who had spent five years as Artistic Director of the Edinburgh Festival and who had also held administrative posts with ITN and with the Scottish National Orchestra 1964-72. Ponsonby was not a 'progressive' in the style of Glock but he was, in the best sense of the word, an elitist. He once said, to a magazine editor who had been criticising what he took to be Ponsonby's anti-populist stance, 'Why have something worse when you can have something better?' And he declared himself in favour of making clear statements about objective standards in musical judgments, famously in 1976: 'Beethoven's *Emperor Concerto* is greater than Rachmaninov's *Second*.' He said that he had a duty to educate

public taste on the basis of scholarly consensus. The composers, the conductors and the most eminent critics - in other words, actual practitioners in music - know what is good and what is less than good. On these grounds, Ponsonby once omitted Tchaikovsky's *B Flat Minor Piano Concerto* from a programme and claimed that a distinction must be made, because time available for listening is not infinite, 'between the very popular and the very great.'

In accordance with these intellectual presuppositions, Ponsonby sought to inform the audiences about music which, he said, quoting George Santayana, should never be 'merely a drowsy reverie punctuated by emotional shocks.' To this end he instituted Pre-Prom Talks, usually at the Royal College of Art or at the Royal College of Music at 6.30 p.m. before each concert. And in his first season, 1974, Ponsonby engaged his predecessor, Glock, to appear as a performer at the piano in Mozart's Quartet in *E Flat K.493.*

New works were played regularly, as under Glock, and some of the most outstanding of these include Henza's opera *The Raft of the Medusa,* which has become a modern classic, Messiaen's *Turangalila Symphony,* Peter Maxwell-Davies' *The Martyrdom of St. Magnus* and Britten's *War Requiem.* Among these 'best' were examples of what many regarded as 'less than the best' and a few follies such as *Twelve Hours of Sunset,* David Bedford's tone poem based on the idea of an aeroplane travelling west and some electronic music including John Taverner's *Ultimos Ritos* which featured tape-recorders.

1977 was the year of the Queen's Silver Jubilee and also the fiftieth anniversary of the BBC's taking over the Promenade concerts. Fittingly, the season began with three concerts of English music - Purcell, Elgar, Vaughan Williams and Walton. Ponsonby admitted in 1977 that, if it came to a choice, he favoured works by living British composers before those by contemporary foreigners. Also in 1977, the BBC importantly confirmed its judgment that the Proms should be the final responsibility of one person. Robert Simpson, for thirty years a Music Producer in the BBC as well as being one of the greatest of living composers, referred to this principle as 'Tyranosaurus Reith' or that of 'benevolent dictatorship tempered by assassination' - by which he meant to insist that the 'one person' holding final responsibility should do so for a limited term and not for life or until retirement.

There were sadnesses in Ponsonby's years of tenure as in 1976 when the opening concert of Beethoven's *Missa Solemnis,* which Rudolf Kempe was to have conducted became Kempe's own memorial concert. Kempe had been appointed Chief Conductor of the BBC Symphony Orchestra as recently as 1975 in succession to Boulez. In the same year the distinguished exponent of music, David Munrow, was engaged to conduct two notable performances but he committed suicide, aged thirty-three.

Ponsonby promoted BBC regional orchestras to Prom performances and not before time according to their members. For as long as anyone can remember, the BBC Northern Symphony Orchestra, based in Manchester, has referred to the BBC S.O. as the BBC *Southern* Symphony Orchestra!

Except perhaps for a few wilderness years after the Second World War, the Promenade concerts have retained their character and remained true to the original vision of Newman and Wood. The involvement of a large organisation like the BBC has meant enormous technical changes, and the subsequent innovations brought about by continent-wide, and occasionally worldwide, television links have produced even greater evolution and change. But at the heart the purpose remains what Newman said it was all those years ago: 'the creation of a public for classical and modern music.'

The Proms Today

"The days of dubious intonation and questionable scholarship are over!"

© Hulton Detsch Collection Ltd.

The spectacle of distinguished members of the BBC Symphony Orchestra playing *Colonel Bogey* in the street outside Broadcasting House and continuing to blow raspberries at the Corporation's senior management would not appear to be the best curtain-raiser to a new season of Promenade concerts. But that scene was the inauspicious beginning to the 1980 series.

The background to the fiasco was partly the Government's refusal to allow the television licence fee to rise sufficiently to cover expenditure. Consequently, the BBC planned cuts in its budget amounting to £130 million and, included in this sum, was £500,000 to be lopped off the £6.5 million spent annually on musicians.

The musicians saw this as a betrayal because the BBC had promised, as far back as 1969, 'to maintain the orchestras beyond the strict needs of broadcasting.' Now, in 1980, it was proposed to disband five of the eleven orchestras and, as a

prelude to this, the BBC sent dismissal notices to 172 players. All the BBC musicians went on strike on 1st June, a matter of weeks before the Proms were due to begin.

Management policy was being conducted with the most unbelievable crassness: for example, the announcement of the disbanding of the Scottish Symphony Orchestra was made at the press conference called to publicise that season's Proms! 'The Scottish' were programmed to play the seventh concert! These actions brought out the whole of the Musicians' Union on strike against the BBC. The Corporation was intransigent, even bloodyminded, and announced: 'The BBC is prepared to sacrifice the Proms rather than drop the plan to disband five orchestras. If the Musicians' Union chooses not to allow broadcasting of the Proms, there will be no Proms.' But the BBC managers faced unprecedented and universal outrage and opposition. The entire International Federation of

Musicians pledged its support for the threatened orchestra. Picket-lines shone with luminaries including such unlikely hotheads as Lady Barbirolli, Sir Lennox Berkeley, Sir Geraint Evans and Sir Charles Groves. There was a three-and-a-half hours debate in the House of Commons during which Anthony Hopkins conducted an orchestra in a performance of Handel's *Water Music* from a barge on the Thames.

Norman Del Mar handed in a petition containing half a million signatures and Bryan Magee criticised the philistinism of the BBC's 'management classes' during the parliamentary debate. Robert Simpson, the leading composer and the most distinguished music producer in the BBC, resigned, '... out of growing disquiet and dwindling respect. I can no longer work for the BBC without a profound sense of betrayal of most of the values I and many others believe in; and its management includes elements whose authority I cannot accept without shame.'

The Managing Director of BBC Radio Aubrey Singer was especially targeted by the protestors as the Musicians' Union wore badges which said 'SAXINGA'. Mutual antipathy hardened into crisis as it became clear there were to be two rival series of Proms - with two rival First Nights!

The opening concert was billed for 18th July and the BBC, for its part, broadcast recorded music. The Musicians' Union had decided that the BBC Symphony Orchestra would stage an alternative First Night 'live' at Alexandra Palace. There was yet more drama as Alexandra Palace burned to the ground on the very day when the M.U. made their announcement. Wembley Conference Centre was quickly proposed as the new venue. Janet Baker sat in the audience on that First Night and so did Malcolm Williamson, Master of the Queen's Music, who attended all the Proms. Sir Adrian Boult sent a message of support.

The acrimony intensified and there was widespread despair at the prospect of the demise of a British institution. A violinist was interviewed on ITV and declared, 'We are being governed by accountants and philistines. The Proms are finished.'

The high seriousness of the dispute was at last seen for what it was: a real threat to the very existence of the Promenade concerts but, even more than that, a blow to the cultural esteem of the nation itself. The foreign press were agog.

Upon the recommendation of a House of Commons Select Committee, Lord Goodman met both sides and the sound of heads being knocked together could be heard throughout the land. The result was that most of the proposed cuts were abandoned and all the sizeable orchestras were preserved. Those musicians who were dismissed had their salaries guaranteed by freelance work for the Corporation for five years. On 1st August, the Musicians' Union voted (393-80) to accept the revised proposals and a small orchestra played from the top of a bus outside Broadcating House to signal the end of the dispute. The 'real Proms' started on 7th August .

At the first rehearsal for this concert John Pritchard was conducting. He said, 'In my part of the world when there is something to celebrate we play a really horrible chord.' So the orchestra played two raspberries. That night, Jessye Norman sang in Mahler's Fourth Symphony and the audience also heard Messiaen's *Poems Pour Mi* - a magnificent new beginning.

There were other highlights of that unusual season, including Michael Tippett's *Triple Concerto* and Clifford Curzon's playing of Beethoven's *Emperor Concerto*, for the two hundredth time in his career. Sir Charles Mackerras conducted his first Last Night and paid tribute to 'Fifty glorious years of the BBC Symphony Orchestra.' Sidonie Goossens played

her harp as usual - her sixtieth Last Night.

During the 1980s Robert Ponsonby instituted the practice of having themed series. For example, 1982 had a French theme in which Boulez's novelty *Repons* was played twice. The centenaries of Stravinsky and Grainger were celebrated and the programme announced a 'British Rail travel and Prom ticket bargain.' Ponsonby said, 'Programme suggestions made at a gathering of Prom-goers last September have in several cases been adopted.' In 1983 many people complained about what they regarded as 'the raucousness and idiocy of the Last Night'. The conductor James Loughran was among those who complained.

A plan was made to deter mere 'day-trippers' and the more mindless of the Hooray Henrys: tickets for the Last Night were to be sold on a first-come-first-served basis but only to those who had booked for at least four other concerts. In that same year the Victoria Room in the Royal Albert Hall was restored and used for pre-Prom talks. And the deaths were announced of two musicians particularly associated with the Proms: Sir William Walton and Sir Adrian Boult.

1984 had British music as its theme and this was entirely appropriate in the year which marked fifty years since the deaths of Elgar, Delius and Holst. Also Robert Ponsonby revealed his penchant for two new developments: Early Music and so called 'authentic' performances in which orchestras tried to present music in the style intended by the original composers.

This is now a widely accepted aspect of music-making but at the time it was controversial and it generated such comments as, 'Authentic performances? Oh you mean half the band turns up late and the other half can't play; no vibrato, so the fiddles sound like a cat's choir, and forte pianos wow like the fat soprano in distress of bladder.' Nevertheless, 'authentic' performances became popular.

Robert Ponsonby took the unusual step that year of singling out one composer for an accolade. He wrote in the official programme: 'Most compelling of all is Sir Michael Tippett's *The Mask of Time*, a summation of the personal philosophy of a great composer and a dearly-loved man.'

All the problems of 1980 were forgotten and the Proms were more than ever a truly international music festival. There were visits from the celebrated Boston Symphony Orchestra and from the legendary Vienna Philharmonic whose President later wrote to the Promenaders: 'You applaud us; we fell in love with you.'

1985 presented an American theme and it was also the tercentenary of three of the greatest names in all music: Bach, Handel and Scarlatti. What an annus mirabilis 1685 was! The opening concert was Handel's *Messiah* in Mozart's version. At the end of the season, Robert Ponsonby retired and he was succeeded by John Drummond, though most of the planning for the 1986 season - the centenary of the death of Franz Liszt - had been done by Ponsonby.

In the programme for 1987, Drummond boasted, 'In many civilised countries, the arts shut down for summer. Not so with us.' And he added, somewhat ambiguously, 'Fifty-three out of this year's sixty-six concerts will display a theme associated with enjoyment.' The theme was 'Music and Dance' and one of the best represented of the composers played that year was good old 'Anon'. Leonard Bernstein was a visiting conductor and he was full of compliments for the Prommers: 'this most extraordinary audience.'

Drummond, officially titled Controller, Radio Three, featured five national youth orchestras in 1988 and introduced the theme of 'Words' - i.e. music with a literary background such as *Harold in Italy* after Byron and *Francesca da Rimini*, Tchaikovsky's 1877 symphonic fantasy after Dante. In this season there were sixty-nine

concerts - the most ever and the Proms covered their cost. They also lived up to the best ideals and intentions of Wood and Newman by including a great deal of modern music. Two thirds of all the music played in 1988 was from the 20th century. It was the year of Andrew Davis' first Last Night. 1989 was Sir John Pritchard's last season as conductor of the BBC Symphony Orchestra.

As the Promenade concerts approached their centenary, they increasingly displayed the confidence which comes with maturity, even with venerability. But for excitement and atmosphere to be generated there must always be a ready supply of vigour and the willingness to innovate. Of these qualities there was no shortage. 1990, declared 'themeless' officially, nonetheless specialised in opera production and offered Handel's *Belshazzar,* Gluck's *Orfeo* and Mozart's *Zauberflote* followed by Tippett's *The Ice Break,* Janacek's *Katya Kabanova* and *Noye's Fludde,* the children's opera by Benjamin Britten.

Besides all these huge productions the centenaries of the birth of Frank Martin and Martinu were marked as well as that of Cesar Franck's death. The First Night offered the massive choral and orchestral *Second Symphony, 'The Resurrection'* by Mahler. Of all this enterprise, Anthony Burgess wrote commending 'British boldness ... like getting a whole army out of Dunkirk.'

John Drummond is never afraid to complain at what he sees as short-comings or injustices. In 1991 - the year of the Mozart bi-centenary - he protested because privately-owned seats in the Albert Hall were often left vacant while there were people left outside who would gladly have paid for them. These were the seats which had, he said, 'been purchased for boxing, tennis or whatever.' It may be that the 1991 season was one of the most glorious. Apart from all

the Mozart festivities - *Idomeneo* and *La Clemenza di Tito* were performed - the centenary of Prokofiev was marked by the first British performance of his opera *The Fiery Angel.* All this and the centenary of Sir Arthur Bliss and the 150th anniversary of the birth of Dvorak and a concert In Memoriam Leonard Bernstein by the London Symphony Orchestra. The series opened with Elgar's *The Dream of Gerontius.* The official programme for the concerts, *The Proms Guide* reached sales of 100,000 making it the largest-selling music publication in the world. Visiting orchestras included the Boston Symphony, and the Berlin Philharmonic. The following year John Drummond complained about coughing during the concerts! Andrew Davis was Chief Conductor and the season featured a recently-discovered Walton piece called *Christopher Columbus* to commemorate the discovering of the New World in 1492.

Last year, 1993, opened with a semi-staged performance of Strauss' *Elektra* and Drummond, now with the title of Director, BBC Promenade Concerts, pledged once again his commitment to 'authentic' performances and declared, 'The days of dubious intonation and question-able scholarship are over.' His pronouncements are beginning to have the ex cathedra ring about them! An institution at ease with itself can afford to relax and the season offered Hans Werner Henze's *Requiem* performed at Sunday lunch-time followed by a picnic in the park: *'All welcome.'*

The History Of The Proms

Celebrating 100 Seasons

© BRITISH BROADCASTING CORPORATION

The Promenaders

"How they have loved their Bach, their Beethoven, their Brahms and their Wagner! More than ever I hoped they would in my wildest dreams!"

© Rex Features Ltd.

'When I look down on that sea of faces before me and conduct my great, amateur, untrained choir, I know that I am British. I know that I am in my native London and I know that in *them* the spirit of Horatio Nelson still lives and will never die.' Henry Wood wrote those words about the Promenaders in his autobiography and he always referred to them as 'My beloved Promenaders.' He also paid tribute to their musical understanding while he criticised their casualness, and even untidiness, in matters of dress.

Certainly the phenomenon which is the Promenaders provokes extreme responses. Many - and particularly the Promenaders themselves! - regard them as England's last bright hope, a gathering of intelligent young people who know how to be exuberant without declining into yobbishness, a chorus of enthusiasts who have not allowed cynicism or the debunking spirit of the age to diminish the vision of these islands as the Land of Hope and Glory.

On the other hand, they have been called 'the noisy, the untutored and the unwashed.' Many can bear witness to the last part of that description, or at least can understand how it might have arisen - if they have stood among a couple of thousand swaying bodies on a hot August night. Much of the blame must fall upon the hideously inadequate air conditioning in the Albert Hall. The best the authorities seem to be able to do is to leave a few doors open.

There is a lot of 'Yah!' and 'Jolly golly!' from the Hooray Henrys and - let us avoid the accusation of male chauvinism - the even shriller Hooray Henriettas. Television has made things worse. Some people will do anything to be seen on screen being interviewed in a concert interval by Richard Baker - or so it semed for a few years rather more than a decade ago.

And the Last Night is always something of a riot which many, including representatives of the great and the good and even eminent conductors and soloists themselves, have thought has sometimes been allowed to go too far - to the extent that it detracts from the music and from the sane person's appreciation of the music.

But it must also be said that an audience which has earned the plaudits of such as Kurt Masur, Leonard Bernstein and the President of the Vienna Philharmonic - to say nothing of Arnold Schoenberg himself! - cannot be all bad, or even all *that* bad.

Leave out the lunatic element and the attention-seekers, and the Proms audience is one of the most musically knowledgeable, and certainly among the most musically-tolerant, in the world. True, there is the allegation that some will 'clap anything' - the more avant garde and cacophonous the better - out of the ludicrous and fatuous desire to appear both fashionable and wise. But there have been dozens of occasions, when pretentious and unmusical music has been received in silence; and Henry Wood himself drew attention to some of these occasions, paying tribute to the discernment of the Promenaders as he did so.

And there have been the famous skirmishes involving the Last Night - the leaving out of the Sea Songs or Land of Hope and Glory and similar desecrations. These events are much magnified because they are the sorts of things which a

© Rex Fewatures Ltd

© Hulton Deutsch Collection Ltd.

debased mass media chooses to find newsworthy and, of course, the Last Night with all its toys, trinkets and trimmings is very televisual. There are sometimes complaints that the carnival spirit of the Last Night is too often allowed to interfere with the music on other nights: 'We are fed up with the behaviour of a few people. Verdi's *Requiem* or Mahler's *Third Symphony* are not the place for prearranged shouting between Arena and Gallery' has been the opinion of some staunch Promenaders.

It is at this point in the debate that a little historical context is called for. In our modern age the place of religion and churchly - spirituality has largely given way to the sense that art itself is holy. This has been brought about by the process of secularisation which has been going on throughout the scientific age. So the feeling which were once reserved for religious response are now frequently exhibited at concerts and art galleries; some people speak in tones of hushed awe of 'the theatre' or 'the ballet.'

It was not always so. Musical perfor-mances were not, historically, usually received with such a show of reverence and it was for a long time the practice to treat musicians as the lowest of the class of hired servants. Delight and displeasure were often shown *during*

performances and, in the 20th century, works have been booed off the platform. In this context, the behaviour of the Promenaders is in no way unusual and in many ways it is exemplary.

It is sometimes forgotten that music is exciting, that it does arouse an audience. It is frequently passionate and often downright sensual. It can also be very funny. Are we to stand through all this transport of delight as if we were wax dummies? Our emotions cannot always be constrained by etiquette and the passionless circumscriptions of good taste. But yes, the repeated Yoo-Ha call of 'Heave!' every time the piano lid is raised has become irritating and boring, a cliché - the Albert Hall's equivalent of the TV soap-opera's catch phrase.

There are occasional erruptions of real wit. For example in the 1974 season Thomas Allen fainted while singing *Carmina Burana* and someone from the audience, who happened to know the piece, took his place. The following night, a banner was unleashed in the auditorium which read: A PROMENADER HAS FAINTED. PLEASE ASK ONE OF THE SOLOISTS TO TAKE HIS PLACE.

On another occasion Prince Charles was in attendance. The whole orchestra assembled at the start for the playing of the National Anthem. When this was over, many of the players began to leave the platform because the first piece on the programme was scored for small forces. The few musicians left on the stage looked lost now that most of their colleagues had gone behind. At once there was a cat-called chorus from the Promenaders: 'Now look what your Royal Highness has done!'

In recent years much has been done to deter mere trendies and attention-seekers, people whose main desire is to have it said of them - in the words of Anthony Burgess - 'You was on the telly.' To get a ticket for the Last Night, you now have to buy tickets for at least

© Rex Features Ltd.

five other concerts. And the toys and rattles have been discouraged.

The Promenade concerts do generate a sense of belonging, of being part of the national family, even of corporate identity. One Promenader described the feeling as 'like being in love or eating lots of chocolate.' Friendships struck at concerts sometimes become lifetime attachments and marriages have been made there. Well, it was Shakespeare who began his own most musical play with the lines, 'If music be the food of love, play on ...'

Most of the Promenaders are in their twenties and thirties, they welcome new music and, since Robert Ponsonby's days, they have been consulted annually about what they think goes to make up a good programme.

Many, at considerable financial sacrifice, buy a season ticket and attend every night. This must provide the cheapest and most comprehensive music lesson on offer worldwide.

Wood and Newman desired to democratise music. It should not be only for the well-to-do who could afford a guinea or more for a ticket even as long ago as the 1890s. Those men, visionaries and founders of the modern musical era as they were, wanted music for the millions.

More than fifty years ago Wood said, 'Where else in the world could we see such sights as we see in the Queen's Hall during the months of August and September each year? Hundreds of young men and girls - have you ever noticed the preponderance of young people in the Promenade? - who wander during the interval to sit on the steps of All Souls' Church and discuss the concerto or the quality of some soprano's high-C; who will stand stock still for forty minutes at a stretch in a hall with the thermometer in the high eighties; who will applaud generously and wholeheartedly those whose artistry they appreciate?'

So they are emotional and sometimes the show of emotion exceeds the bounds of drawing-room propriety. So we are in a concert hall and not a funeral parlour and we are priveleged to listen to the most exciting sound in the known universe: that of a symphony orchestra off like a pack of hounds in pursuit of, as it might be, Beethoven's *Eroica*. It is not a moment to want to remain in one's seat.

Of course some expressed emotion is only for show and it can be effete and affected with a cringe factor of a hundred. But there will always remain the real thing which cannot be faked. Barrie Hall has made the appropriate distinction for us:

'"If people cry, why should they not laugh?" said Richard Strauss of his *Don Quixote*. What gives music, or drama, or literature this power to transmit emotion? "It is not strange that sheep's guts should haul souls out of men's bellies?" wrote Shakespeare.

'But how do the tears and the laughter get in? The composer was not laughing or crying; he was wrestling with form. Nor is the performer, he is concentrating on technique. With a poet's insight, Peter Porter approaches the heart of it: "When there is no technique, emotion comes out as embarrassment. When there is technique, it comes out as the original emotion." 'We may never get closer than that.'

The defining characteristic of the Proms and of the Promenaders is the fact that for them music is permanent. It does not stop when the concert is over. The planners are at once

planning the next series. The Promenaders are whistling tunes from the concert they have just heard and talking avidly about the next. Nowhere is this animation more keenly or more closely observed than in the pavement queue outside the concert hall. This is an ambience rich in anecdotes.

One such anecdote is recounted by a devoted Promenader standing in the concert queue immediately before the Second World War. He said, 'It was a hot night and we were being serenaded by an out-of-work violinist, busking. He wasn't very good and consequently there weren't many coins in his hat.

'Suddenly, an imposing man stepped out of the queue and said; "Here, let me see what I can do." He took the beggar's fiddle and played a virtuoso piece quite sparkingly. Dozens of coins were then thrown into the beggar's hat. And it turned out that the imposing volunteer fiddler was a bishop who had just returned to England after missionary work in Africa.'

That story says much about the sympathies of the typical Proms audience!

It was the Promenaders who made a happy man out of Henry Wood. Their response was his reward. Towards the end of his life he said, 'And how they have *listened* all these forty-odd years! How still they have stood! How they have loved their Bach, their Beethoven, their Brahms and their Wagner! More than ever I hoped they would in my wildest dreams!'

And how they listen still.

© Rex Fewatures Ltd

Epilogue:
Principals and Personalities of the Proms

T his section must be prefaced with an apology for it is bound to give offence. The problem is, of course, that in a hundred years of concerts hundreds of internationally celebrated soloists and thousands of fine orchestral musicians have made their contribution and it is impossible to mention them all.

The following selection is almost completely arbitrary - but not quite. Space has been given to Sir Malcolm Sargent because he was the conductor most closely identified in the public mind with the Proms, after Wood himself.

The rest of the choice of principals is intended to give a flavour, an indication, of the great variety of characters who have appeared in all these years. It follows that omission from this short roll-call does not imply any musician's unimportance. Both those whom have been mentioned, and the great many more who have not, have played their part in providing the greatest series of concerts which the world has ever seen.

SIR MALCOLM SARGENT (1895-1967)	EILEEN JOYCE (1912 - 1991)
DAME ISOBEL BAILLIE (1895-1983)	HERBERT VON KARAJAN (1908 - 1989)
DAME JANET BAKER (1933 -)	RUDOLF KEMPE (1910 - 1976)
SIR JOHN BARBIROLLI (1899 - 1970)	SIR PETER MAXWELL DAVIES (1934 -)
DANIEL BARENBOIM (1942 -)	SIR YEHUDI MENUHIN (1916 -)
SIR THOMAS BEECHAM (1879-1961)	BENNO MOISEIWITSCH (1890 - 1963)
SIR ADRIAN BOULT (1889 - 1983)	JOHN OGDON (1937 - 1989)
DENNIS BRAIN (1921 - 1957)	SIR PETER PEARS (1910 - 1986)
BENJAMIN BRITTEN (1913 - 1976)	JACQUELINE DU PRÉ (1945 - 87)
PIERRE BOULEZ (1925 -)	ANDRE PREVIN (1929 -)
FERRUCHIO BUSONI (1866 - 1924)	MSTISLAV ROSTROPOVICH (1927 -)
BASIL CAMERON (1884 - 1975)	GENNADI ROZHDESTVENSKY (1931 -)
PABLO CASALS (1876 - 1973)	ARNOLD SCHOENBERG (1874 - 1951)
SIR CLIFFORD CURZON (1907 - 1982)	ETHEL SMYTH (1858 - 1944)
SIR COLIN DAVIS (1927 -)	SOLOMON (1902 - 1988)
KATHLEEN FERRIER (1912 - 1953)	SIR GEORG SOLTI (1912 -)
KIRSTEN FLAGSTADT (1895 - 1962)	LEOPOLD STOKOWSKI (1882 - 1977)
EDVARD GRIEG (1843 - 1907)	RICHARD STRAUSS (1864 - 1949)
GLYNDEBOURNE FESTIVAL OPERA	RICHARD TAUBER (1892-1948)
SIR EUGENE GOOSSENS (1893-1962)	DAME MAGGIE TEYTE (1888 - 1976)
PERCY GRAINGER (1882 - 1961)	DAME EVA TURNER (1892 - 1990)
BERNARD HAITINK (1929 -)	RALPH VAUGHAN WILLIAMS (1872 - 1958)
DAME MYRA HESS (1890-1966)	SIR WILLIAM WALTON (1902 - 1983)

SIR MALCOLM SARGENT (1895-1967)

© Hulton Deutsch Collection Ltd.

In the hierarchy and mythology of the Promenade concerts, Sir Malcolm Sargent stands second only to Wood himself. 'Flash Harry' was the nickname given to him by orchestral players and it was said that he was famous for his smart suits and exuberant smalltalk. He was not generally liked by players. They found his bumptiousness and perpetual self-advertisement hard to tolerate. And yet he was a huge favourite with the Promenaders and a household name nationwide - perhaps, we should say, one of the first 'media personalities.'

He was the popular audience's idea of a conductor: flamboyant, handsome and dashing, suave as a diplomat and with an upper class accent and a generally aristocratic mien. Yet his father was a coal merchant in Stamford, Lincolnshire.

Harold Malcolm Watts Sargent was born in that town in the same year that Henry Wood began the Proms. As a boy he sang in the local choir and learned piano and organ. He was precocious and ambitious and he went to be pupil to the organist at Peterborough Cathedral; by the time he was nineteen, he was organist to the parish church of Melton Mowbray. He took his Bachelor of Music degree at Durham in 1914 and, after brief military service in the First World War, his Doctorate in 1919.

In 1923 Sargent joined the teaching staff at the Royal College of Music and he became Chief Conductor of the Robert Mayer Children's Concerts in 1924. He was involved with Beecham's LPO from 1932 onwards and he toured with that orchestra during the Blitz. He was appointed Chief Conductor of the Hallé Orchestra (1939-42) and of the Liverpool Philharmonic (1942-48), specialising in operetta and oratorio. As he himself said, 'My career has been based on two Ms: *Messiah* and *Mikado'*.

His early career was blighted by a bout of TB between 1933 and 1934 but apart from that interruption his energy never flagged and he was the outstanding British choral conductor of his time. It was said that choirs gave him the unstinting devotion whch was not always forthcoming from orchestral players. He conducted the Royal Choral Society and the Huddersfield Choral Society for twenty-five years and, among his notable achievements, gave the first performance of *Belshazzar's Feast,* by William Walton, at the Leeds Festival in 1931.

He was Conductor of the BBC Symphony Orchestra from 1950 to 1957 and Chief Conductor of the Promenade concerts from 1948 until his death nineteen years later. His knighthood came in 1947 and in 1957 he was awarded the Gold Medal of the Royal Philharmonic Society.

Some musicians of very pure sensitivity and serious intent could not warm to Sargent: they took to heart Maurice Johnstone's jibe that music was 'only Sargent's shop-window.' And indeed he could be a frenetic and irritating self-publicist. He was part of the BBC's very popular celebrity panel *The Brains Trust* and he liked to be thought of as an all round genius - a sort of Renaissance Man in a Saville Row suit. He loved to play for 'crowned heads of the nations' and to be called 'Britain's Ambassador for Music.'

The Times obituarist wrote of him: 'As a public figure he was celebrated for his sartorial elegance and his seemingly infallible ability to converse knowledgeably and wittily on all manner of topics ...he was sometimes the victim of his own versatility and of his passion for efficiency and for his taste which was moulded by the Victorian cathedral tradition.'

His arrogance annoyed the more learned and experienced of orchestral players as, for example, when he made cuts

to Schubert's *'Great' C major Symphony*. Even the obituary could not omit mention of this side of Sargent's personality: 'He became impatient of music from which he could not at once draw an effect; this led him to retouch scores of the past with a self-will which scholarly musicians could not condone.'

His taste was certainly conservative and his characteristic utterances make him seem as if he were a Victorian man-about-town fallen upon us through a time-warp. It is not going too far to say that he hated the avant garde and that he neither understood nor tried to understand the music of the Second Viennese School, of Barrok and Hindemith and even of Stravinsky, Britten and Michael Tippett.

His tastes are best revealed in his choice of programme while he was Chief Conductor of the Proms. He played only one hundred and fifty new works between 1947 and 1959 and most of these were 'middle of the road, traditional' in style. There were no novelties at all in 1952. And Sargent summed up his own musical assessment of twentieth century composers in a sentence: 'Posterity will say that, of composers now living, Sibelius is first and Vaughan Williams is second.' Sixty years on, posterity says no such thing.

He constantly strove for instant effect, saying, 'What is of importance to me is whether they'll come and hear a piece of music, whether I dare put it on again; whether it will make money or not.' You may admire his sense of responsibility to the consumer but his attitude and policy are a world away from Wood's and Newman's passion to educate the public by playing the familiar and the unfamiliar - in short, by playing everything.

He said, 'The music of the moderns is intellectual manufacture. It's not like the classics. Some people get the same stimulus from it as playing chess. It's not like looking at a blue sea or a blue sky.'

Some modern music *is* emotionally arid, all disembodied mind as it were; but there are modern classics which, as experience has shown, can move audiences to tears as well as ever Schubert, Mendelssohn or Wagner did. Moreover, there was the historical side to Sargent's character and it is well-described by Ates Orga: 'His arguments and quarrels with orchestral players invariably left him in a weak state, in floods of tears and with something akin to a persecution complex.'

Everything about him was high wire, or like an explosion waiting to happen. When he played the piano, the explosion did happen and another of his nicknames among musicians was Mal the Banger. A contemporary wrote: 'Sargent displayed a frank enjoyment of fame and success which a more cautious person would have concealed, not from modesty but from fear of ridicule.'

His life also contained tragedy. In 1944 his daughter Pamela died of polio - a bereavement from which Sargent never fully recovered. Perhaps much of his exuberance was forced gaiety and a mask covering the heart's sorrow? At any rate, it was said, 'He was a restless man for whom dancing until dawn after a concert seemed to be a necessary relaxation. And he had a natural inclination to spend freely.'

Sargent was not, then, an intellectual's musician, or even a musician's musician - except among the choirs who adored him - but he did make the Proms live in the life of the nation in the gloomy postwar period when the whole institution of these great concerts might have fallen.

If he achieved this by flamboyance and bravado ... well, each man must work in his own way and according to the measure of his own gifts; and he *did* achieve the popular success of the Proms.

And on 3rd October 1967 when he died, the public shed profuse and genuine tears for at 'Flash Harry'.

DAME ISOBEL BAILLIE (1895-1983)

She was born in Hawick, Scotland and she became one of the most famous sopranos of the century, particulary in oratorio, and she gave more than a thousand performances of *Messiah*.

Wood described her as 'a young and pretty girl with masses of golden hair and a voice equally golden. In all my work with her, I have never found her anything but note-perfect - whether in *The Wife From Bath* or Brahm's *'Requiem.'*

She gave a particulary brilliant performance in the finale of Beethoven's *Ninth Symphony* at a Prom in 1932.

DAME JANET BAKER (1933 -)

Dame Janet Baker, born in Yorkshire, is a mezzo soprano with a great reputation for singing works by late romantic composers. She has sung Mahler's *Kindertotenlieder* at the Proms and in 1974 she sang the lead in the first Proms performance of *Savriti* by Gustav Holst.

SIR JOHN BARBIROLLI (1899 - 1970)

Born in London, of Franco-Italian origin, Barbirolli succeeded Toscanini as conductor of the New York Philharmonic Orchestra in 1937 before returning to England to be Chief Conductor of the Hallé Orchestra from 1943-58. He was one of the finest, most deeply intelligent, conductors of his generation and Vaughan Williams always referred to him as 'glorious John.'

In 1958 Barbirolli provided a celebration concert at the Proms: 'A replica of the first concert given by the Hallé Society in 1858.' He conducted frequently for the Proms in the 1950s but not as frequently as the BBC Management would have liked; for he was usually engaged with his beloved Hallé Orchestra.

Sir Charles Groves conducted Barbirolli's memorial concert at the Proms on 28th August 1970.

DANIEL BARENBOIM (1942 -)

He was a child prodigy and he learned all the Beethoven piano sonatas in a single summer when he was seventeen as a way of deriving relief from his unhappiness following a love affair. He has made many appearances at the Proms, particularly with Zubin Mehta and the Israel Philharmonic Orchestra. He was married to the cellist Jacqueline du Pré who died from multiple sclerosis at the age of forty-two in 1987.

Barenboim is an intellectual, a philosophically-minded musician, firmly believing that human, psychological difficulties could be solved by understanding and performing music.

SIR THOMAS BEECHAM (1879-1961)

He was the son of Sir Joseph Beecham, the famous 'pill' millionaire. Sir Thomas was Principal Conductor and Artistic Director at Covent Garden and in 1943 he conducted the Metropolitan Opera in New York. He was a great champion of Delius when that composer's work was out of fashion and he was a tremendous wit and raconteur. He once called Herbert Von Karajan 'a sort of musical Malcom Sargent.'

Sir Adrian Boult

© Hulton Deutsch Collection Ltd.

He conducted popular pieces - his so called 'lollipops' - at a Promenade concert on 9th October 1915 and he appeared again only twice at a Prom, in the Diamond Jubilee year 1954.

BLACK DYKE MILLS BAND AND GRIMETHORPE COLLIERY BAND

Yorkshire coalminers' famous ensembles who performed Elgar, Holst, Grainger and Harrison Birtwistle's *Grimethorpe Aria* at a Prom in 1974. In 1975 they returned to repeat their success with a Gilbert and Sullivan programme.

SIR ADRIAN BOULT (1889 - 1983)

Adrian Boult conducted the City of Birmingham Orchestra from 1924 until 1930 when he was appointed Musical Director at the BBC and conductor of the BBC Symphony Orchestra. His influence on the musical policy of the BBC and the Proms was considerable, particularly his support for English composers.

He shared the burden of conducting with Wood and Cameron and conducted for the Jubilee Concert in 1944.

DENNIS BRAIN (1921 - 1957)

He was quite simply the best horn player of the century and his performance of the Richard Strauss *Horn Concerto* was the highlight of the 1950 season. He was killed in a car crash on his way home from the Edinburgh Festival in 1957.

THE HISTORY OF THE PROMS

© Hulton Deutsch Collection Ltd.

BENJAMIN BRITTEN (1913 - 1976)

He was Britain's leading twentieth century composer, a musician who had completely assimilated the innovations of the serialists and the continental avant garde but who also had a commanding grasp of the whole classical tradition as well as the church music of the great renaissance composers. His great favourite was Purcell and he conducted *Fairy Queen* at the Proms in 1971. Britten himself is the greatest English opera composer since Purcell and his *Peter Grimes* (1945) consolidated his worldwide reputation as a musical dramatist.

He was soloist in a performance of his *Piano Concerto*, conducted by Wood, in 1938. Sadlers Wells gave a performance of his *Gloriana* (the opera composed for the Coronation in 1953) at a sixtieth birthday concert for Britten in 1973 at the Proms. His *War Requiem* was performed on 1st August 1963. In 1967, Prince Charles attended a performance of Bach's *St. John Passion* conducted by Britten as part of the Proms season.

Sir Benjamin Britten

PIERRE BOULEZ (1925 -)

He is a French conductor and avant garde composer who rebelled against the conservatism of Stravinsky and Schoenberg! Boulez really understands modern music and his great legacy to the Proms is his making the new sound world of twentieth century music intelligible and accessible to audiences who previously found it to be unapproachable. He became Chief Conductor of the BBC Symphony Orchestra in 1972.

FERRUCHIO BUSONI (1866 - 1924)

Busoni was a child prodigy who never had a lesson from any great master, but he matured into the most spectacular virtuoso among pianists - with the single, possible, exception of Liszt himself. He was an individualist eccentric. For example, he actually believed that he was being more true to the spirit of Mozart when he played the notes of a piano piece otherwise than Mozart's scoring!

Every amateur pianist knows that the playing of fast scale passages presents one of the most testing challenges of technique. Busoni played fast scale passages in contrary motion - up and down the piano with both hands - in octaves. He always sat on a long stool at the keyboard so that, as he once told Henry Wood, 'I can shift a couple of inches in either direction.'

Basil Cameron

© Hulton Deutsch Collection Ltd.

He was also something of a satirist. Whenever, riding in a coach, he passed the Royal Academy of Music, he would raise his hat in mock respect. Wood adored him but he confessed to being terrified whenever Busoni met up with Sibelius: the two of them would go about town for days and nights on end eating and drinking in the restaurants and clubs. 'They were like a couple of irresponsible schoolboys.' And rather anxiety-provoking if the great pianist was down to play a concerto in the Queen's Hall! Busoni's first appearance at the Promenade concerts was on 24th November 1900 and, according to Wood, it was an event which 'thrilled all musical London.'

BASIL CAMERON (1884 - 1975)

Cameron played the violin in the Queen's Hall Orchestra in 1908 and went on to make his reputation in America where he became Director of the Seattle Symphony Orchestra after Thomas Beecham. He returned to England in 1938 to conduct the Covent Garden Opera Company and he was one of the principal conductors of the Promenade concerts from 1941 until his retirement in 1964, aged eighty.

Wood said, 'Cameron has a real grip over the orchestra and a knowledge of the repertoire and tradition second to none. I admit he takes a bit of knowing and have come

to the conclusion he is a very shy, sensitive man, but his music is right.' Cameron conducted the first Prom after the war, the year following Wood's death, and he was a favourite with the Albert Hall audiences. More than most, Cameron seems to have been the victim of the mood swings of the BBC bureaucrats, moving in and out of favour according to changes of leadership in the Music Department.

He was a careful, thorough man, a musician to his fingertips; but his calm and rather diffident nature sometimes led to his being considered ineffectual - but only by the undiscerning. Certainly his personality was a contrast with that of Sargent. A review of Cameron's directing of *Rite of Spring* in 1947 indicates the sort of reaction he tended to provoke: 'Cameron negotiated this novelty successfully, if with something less than complete abandon.'

PABLO CASALS (1876 - 1973)

Casals was one of the greatest cellists of all time and he appeared at the Proms in 1911 to play Dvorak's *Concerto in B minor*. He was fidgety and he had strong views about how the orchestra should accompany him in a concerto. Wood said, 'He has a habit of turning round to the orchestra and hissing them down if they dare to make too strong a crescendo.' His tone was universally regarded as exquisite. Casals founded the Barcelona Orchestra in 1919 and he conducted it until the outbreak of the Spanish Civil War in 1936 when he left Spain, never to return.

SIR CLIFFORD CURZON (1907 - 1982)

He entered the Royal Academy of Music when he was twelve and made his solo piano debut in Bach's *Triple Concerto* under Henry Wood and he played Schubert at a Prom in 1925. Wood wrote: 'Has the *Wanderer Fantaisie* ever been played more poetically?' He also played the Piano Concerto for the Delius memorial concert in 1934.

SIR COLIN DAVIS (1927 -)

Sir Colin became Chief Conductor of the BBC Symphony Orchestra (1961-71) and, as Musical Director at Covent Garden (1971-86), he won an international reputation for his productions of *The Ring*. He took over the role of Principal Conductor of the Proms after Sargent's death in 1967.

He objected to 'the jingoism, patriotic flag waving and exhibitionism' of the Last Night. He played a version of *Sailors' Hornpipe* in 5/8 time to confuse the rhythmic stamping of the Promenaders! But he became very popular and a frequent cry at the Proms was, 'We want Colin!'

Sir Colin Davis

© Hulton Deutsch Collection Ltd.

Kathleen Ferrier

© Hulton Deutsch Collection Ltd.

KATHLEEN FERRIER (1912 - 1953)

Ferrier was one of the greatest contraltos of the century. She was born in Higher Walton, Lancashire and began training as a singer only after winning a prize at a local music festival in 1940. (She had originally trained as a pianist). She had a voice so mellow and resonant that in many people it evoked spiritual experience. Her triumphs were chiefly in passionate roles concerned with love and death: Lucretia in Britten's *The Rape of Lucretia*. Orpheus in *Orfeo* by Gluck and messenger of farewell in Mahler's *Das Lied Von Der Erde* which she sang at the first Edinburgh Festival in 1947.

Kathleen Ferrier made her Proms debut with Brahms' *Alto Rhapsody* in the same year and she was asked to repeat this success in 1948. She sang again Brahms' *Four Serious Songs* in 1949.

She was known and loved by everyone who owned a wireless set for her heartbreaking rendering of *Che Faro* ('What is Life?') from *Orfeo*. She died of cancer at the height of her powers in 1953.

KIRSTEN FLAGSTADT (1895 - 1962)

Legendary Wagnerian soprano whose Sieglinde at Bayreuth in 1934 is still remembered with awe. In 1957 she came out of retirement and put on Norwegian national costume to sing the Grieg Fiftieth Anniversary Prom.

EDVARD GRIEG (1843 - 1907)

The Norwegian composer, renowned for *Peer Gynt* and the *Piano Concerto in A minor*, appeared at the Proms in 1906 when he directed his *Bergliot* and *Lyric Suite*. He lodged with Sir Edgar Speyer in Grosvenor Street.

Henry Wood describes Grieg as 'a shy, refined, delicate little man' who lived in almost total seclusion with his wife, a notable linguist, in their country house near Bergen. Debussy referred to Grieg's music as 'bonbons wrapped in snow.'

He toured Europe playing his own piano music and he was well-known for his wit. He was made Knight of the Order of Orange-Nassau and he was very quick to accept the title and the trinkets that went with it, because, as he said, 'Orders and medals are most useful to me in the top layer of my trunk. The customs officials are always so kind to me at the sight of them.'

GLYNDEBOURNE FESTIVAL OPERA

This was founded in East Sussex in 1934 by John Christie (1882-1962) and it presents an annual festival which has become world famous. In 1961 the company performed *Don Giovanni* at the Proms, under John Pritchard conducting the Royal Philharmonic Orchestra. The following year the company returned to present *Cosi Van Tutte*.

They have played regularly at the Proms in recent years.

SIR EUGENE GOOSSENS (1893-1962)

He was a composer and conductor, the most eminent member of a famous musical family. Sir Eugene conducted his own composition *Chinese Variations* in 1913 and his symphonic poem *Perseus* the following year. He had a third successful premiere with *The Eternal Rhythm*. Wood praised his work as 'outstanding' and expressed disappointment when the composer left to work in America.

PERCY GRAINGER (1882 - 1961)

Australian pianist who studied under Busoni and championed the music of Delius. He wrote some pieces of high class pastiche and modern intonation such as *Handel In The Strand* and 'lollipops' like *Country Gardens*. He played

Tchaikovsky's *B' minor Piano Concerto* at a Prom on 17th August 1904 and Wood said, 'I preferred him to play Grieg even though his playing of the Tchaikovsky was energetic and clean-fingured.'

There is a piano roll of Grainger's performance of the Grieg *A minor Piano Concerto*.

BERNARD HAITINK (1929 -)

His first appearance with the Amsterdam Concertgebouw was in 1956 and he became its Chief Conductor in 1964. He became Principal Conductor of the London Philharmonic Orchestra in 1967; subsequently being appointed Musical Director at Glyndebourne and, in 1987, Musical Director of the Royal Opera House, Covent Garden. He is one of the finest conductors in the world, regarded particularly for his interpretations of Mahler's symphonies. In 1967 he brought *The Resurrection Symphony* (No. 2 in C minor) to the Proms and he conducted a memorial concert for Shostakovich in 1975.

His exhilarating direction of Bruckner's *Fifth Symphony* in 1980 helped restore cheerfulness and élan to the Proms after the musicians' strike.

DAME MYRA HESS (1890-1966)

Dame Myra was a pianist whose name had passed into the folklore of the twentieth century in Britain for her performances at lunchtime concerts in the National Gallery during the Blitz. She was responsible for the legendary interpretation of Bach's *Cantata No. 147, Jesu, Joy of Man's Desiring*. But her Proms debut was as a young woman of eighteen, playing Liszt's *E flat Piano Concerto*, conducted by Wood. She was an enormous favourite with the Promenaders. Wood said in 1938, 'Her musicianship has matured - whose does not in thirty years? - but she *was* the great artist then.'

Wood gave his musical services for charity many times, but only once for a solo artist's concert: that was for Myra Hess.

EILEEN JOYCE (1912 - 1991)

Australian concert pianist discovered by Percy Grainger. She studied under Artur Schnabel and in 1930 she was introduced to Sir Henry Wood. In 1934 she played at the Last Night: Busoni's *Indian Fantasy* and in 1949 she performed John Ireland's *Piano Concerto* for the composer's seventieth birthday.

HERBERT VON KARAJAN (1908 - 1989)

Brilliant and idiosyncratic conductor, controversial for his having joined the Nazi Party in 1933. He conducted with the great European orchestras: The Berlin Philharmonic and the Vienna State Opera. He was also a gifted interpreter of opera and associated with Bayreuth.

At a 'Fanfare for Europe' winter Prom in 1973, Karajan conducted the Berlin Philharmonic Orchestra in Beethoven's *Fourth* and *Fifth Symphonies.*

RUDOLF KEMPE (1910 - 1976)

Conductor of the Dresden and Munich orchestras and a renowned interpreter of Wagner's *Ring*. From 1961 he was Principal Conductor of the Royal Philharmonic Orchestra. He conducted a magnificent and tumultuously received performance of Strauss' *Ein Heldenleben* in 1974 and he was made Chief Conductor of the BBC Symphony Orchestra in 1975. He was to have conducted Beethoven's *Missa Solemnis* to open the 1976 season but he died and the concert was given as his memorial.

SIR PETER MAXWELL DAVIES (1934 -)

Sir Peter is a composer of symphonies with rich harmonic texture and he also writes in a more sparse and pared-down style music reflecting the austere environment of the Orkneys where he lives for part of every year. He conducted his *Fantasia On An In Nomine of John Taverner* at the Proms in 1962.

His chamber group the Fires of London gave a performance of Schoenberg's *Pierrot Lunaire* (with the soloist Mary Thomas in Pierrot costume) in 1972.

SIR YEHUDI MENUHIN (1916 -)

He made his debut at the age of seven with the San Francisco Symphony Orchestra and he was coached by Elgar himself to play that composer's *Violin Concerto* in 1932. Sir Yehudi played the concerto during the 1946 season. His school at Stoke D'Abernon for children who are musically gifted is renowned throughout the world.

© Hulton Deutsch Collection Ltd.

*John
Ogdon*

BENNO MOISEIWITSCH
(1890 - 1963)

He was born in Odessa and he won the Rubinstein pianists' prize at the age of nine. He made his first Proms appearance in 1914 and he was a frequent performer between the wars. In 1958, the First Night honoured Robert Newman (born 1858) and Moiseiwitsch, aged sixty-eight, played piano solos in the second half.

JOHN OGDON
(1937 - 1989)

British pianist famous for having shared the Tchaikovsky Prize with Ashkenazy in 1962. He played Rachmaninov's *Third Piano Concerto* with the USSR State Orchestra. The Russians invaded Czechoslovakia on the same day as their first Prom! He had made his Proms debut in 1959, playing Liszt's *Piano Concerto No.1*

SIR PETER PEARS
(1910 - 1986)

British tenor who formed a lifelong partnership with Sir Benjamin Britten. He created the title role in *Peter Grimes* in 1945 and went on to sing the lead in all Britten's operas. He was famous for his singing of the Evangelist in Bach's *St. Matthew Passion*. With Britten, he founded the Aldeburgh Festival in 1948.

His Proms appearances include Britten's *Nocturne* in 1960. Before that he had sung in Britten's *Serenade for Tenor, Horn and Strings* (with Dennis Brain playing the horn) in Coronation year and in *Les Illuminations* also by Britten in 1945.

JACQUELINE DU PRÉ (1945 - 1987)

She studied the cello with the century's three great masters: Casals, Rostropovich and Tortelier and made her debut, aged sixteen. She first played at the Proms in 1962 and again in 1963 when she performed the Elgar *Cello Concerto* - a work into which she poured intense emotionality and which she subsequently made her own. Her progressive illness tragically forced her to give up concert performance in 1972.

ANDRE PREVIN (1929 -)

He is a German born American conductor and composer, conductor of the London Symphony Orchestra (1968-79). He has composed musicals and film scores and he writes entertainingly about music and life. Previn conducted Sir William Walton's seventieth birthday concert in 1972.

But perhaps he is even more renowned for having been the conductor when Thomas Allen was singing in *Carmina Burana* in 1974. It was a hot night and the Albert Hall was even more stuffy than usual. Allen collapsed in a faint and his place was taken by an amateur singer, Patrick McCarthy, who emerged from the audience to save the day.

*Kath...
Ferrier...
P...
Pe...*

©
D...
Collecti...

MSTISLAV ROSTROPOVICH (1927 -)

The Russian cellist is regarded as one of the century's greatest performers on that instrument. It is recalled how he was moved to tears at a Promenade concert in 1968 when he was playing the Czech composer, Dvorak's *Cello Concerto* with the State Orchestra of the USSR - just as the Soviets were invading Czechoslovakia.

GENNADI ROZHDESTVENSKY (1931 -)

Conductor of the Moscow Radio Orchestra who became Chief Conductor of the BBC Symphony Orchestra in 1978. In his first concert he conducted Britten's *Diversions on a Theme*, with Mrs. Rozhdestvensky (Victoria Postnikova) at the piano.

ARNOLD SCHOENBERG (1874 - 1951)

Schoenberg stands in the same relationship to modern music as Bach stood to the classical period: he is the most influential composer of the twentieth century, a genius who twice in his career revolutionised the very principles upon which the art of musical composition is based.

An admirer of Wagner and Mahler, - he wrote Mahler's obituary in 1911, beginning with the words, 'Gustav Mahler was a saint' - Schoenberg invented first so called 'atonal' music and then the compositional strategy known as 'twelve tone.' His concerts in his new styles were often interrupted by boos and even by riots so that he and his associates - among them Alban Berg, Anton Webern and Alexander Zemlinsky - founded The Society For the Private Performance of Music.

Schoenberg conducted his *Five Orchestral Pieces* at a Promenade concert in January 1914 and he subsequently wrote a letter of appreciation to Robert Newman from Berlin - 'for the careful way with which you played in my rehearsals and the performance. I must say that it was the first time since Gustav Mahler that I heard such music played again as a musician of culture demands.'

He ended his letter with an ominous premonition of the First World War: 'I experienced a great pleasure, which has only been troubled by the sad knowledge that with us things are not everywhere as they should be.'

ETHEL SMYTH (1858 - 1944)

English composer and suffragette, Dame Ethel Smyth was the first woman to conduct the Queen's Hall orchestra at a Promenade concert. She wrote large operas such as *The Wreckers* (1906) and *The Boatswain's Mate* (1916): also the battle song of the Women's Social and Political Union - *The March of the Women.* She was imprisoned for three months for her extra-musical activities.

Dame Ethel was certainly what is known as 'a character' and Wood described her as 'a law unto herself.' He said that she was fond of making last minute alterations to her compositions even to the extent of slipping into the

Jacqueline DuPré

© Hulton Deutsch Collection Ltd.

orchestral pit minutes before the performance and attaching notices of amendment to the musicians' scores!

When she conducted at the Proms in 1913, Dame Ethel found that Wood's baton was too long for her liking - so she snapped it in two, threw away one half and conducted with the other!

SOLOMON (1902 - 1988)

His full name was Solomon Cutner and he was born in London. He was a child prodigy as a pianist. Wood refers to his first appearance at the Proms on 24th August 1914. 'This child of eleven appealed tremendously to the audience with his winning, soulful eyes, his little silk shirt and short knickers. His performance of the *Second* of Beethoven's piano concertos was amazing.

SIR GEORG SOLTI (1912 -)

Sir Georg was born in Budapest and studied originally to be a pianist at the Franz Liszt Academy. He made his conducting debut in 1938 in a performance of *Le Nozze Di Figaro* with the Budapest Opera. He was Musical Director at Covent Garden (1961-71) and he brought many opera performances to the Proms, notably *Das Rheingold* in 1970. He became conductor of the Chicago Symphony Orchestra in 1969 which he brought to the Albert Hall in the 1978 season. He had previously said to his orchestra: 'You wait till we get to the Proms: I will show you an audience!' They earned a tumultuous reception for Michael Tippett's *Fourth Symphony*.

LEOPOLD STOKOWSKI (1882 - 1977)

Born in the East End of London, he later lived in America where he became Conductor of the Philadelphia Symphony Orchestra (1912-36), the New York Philharmonic (1946-50) and the Houston Symphony Orchestra (1955-60). He was a showman and popular publicist for music, appearing in films such as *A Hundred Men and a Girl* (1937) and *Fantasia* (1940). Wood criticised Stokowski's orchestral transcriptions of Bach's organ pieces: 'I always seem to find the organist peeping out.' Stokowski conducted Mahler's *Resurrection Symphony* at the Proms in 1963 and, aged eighty-four, he gave an exciting performance of Tchaikovsky's *Fifth Symphony* three years later.

RICHARD STRAUSS (1864 - 1949)

Strauss was among the greatest of the late-romantic composers along with Mahler, Elgar and Delius. Wood persuaded him to come to the Proms in 1902 and to conduct his beautiful tone poem *Ein Heldenleben* ('A Hero's Life'). He was tall, with a noble bearing which made everyone remark on how distinguished he looked.

He is celebrated for his tone poems and romantic operas, for the expansive *Alpine Symphony* and, in modern times, for *Also Sprach Zarathustra* - an extract from which provided the theme music for a television film of the moon voyages of the 1960s and 1970s.

Strauss was also a bon viveur and he loved to play cards. Gossips said that he was dominated by his wife, an excitable, talkative woman much given to the hectic social life and expensive shopping expeditions. (It was she whom Henry Wood took into Dickens and Jones in Regent Street to buy knickers).

Although he is chiefly remembered for his compositions, Strauss was also a conductor of genius who succeeded Felix Weingartner as Director of the Royal Opera in Berlin in 1898 - a post which he held until 1918. And, while his music was all burgeoning romanticism, his style of conducting was restricted and pared-down. He kept himself out of the music so that the notes might speak for themselves.

RICHARD TAUBER (1892-1948)

Tauber is well known for his many appearances as 'a light tenor' in the operettas of Franz Lehar and in the 1930s he sang in some popular film musicals. But he was one of the finest singers of Mozart and his performance of *Il Mio Tsoro* from *Don Giovanni* - an aria which requires the prodigiously long sustaining of a note (with embellishments) is legendary.

He made his Proms debut in the 1939 season which was curtailed by the outbreak of war. Wood said Tauber had 'such a caressing voice; none of Caruso's overblowing and squirting out top notes!'

DAME MAGGIE TEYTE (1888 - 1976)

She was chosen by Debussy to play Mélisande in *Pelleas et Mélisande* and she became the most prominent interpreter of French Impressionist music. On the First Night of the 1922 Proms season, she sang *Tatiana's Letter Song* from *Eugen Onegin* by Tchaikovsky, and Mimi's song from *La Boheme* in 1934.

Dame Maggie was a most popular performer and she loved to work with Wood. She said, 'One never refused him. After all, he was Sir Henry Wood and had all the concerts and halls at his disposal.'

DAME EVA TURNER (1892 - 1990)

British soprano (born in Oldham) and Prima Donna of the Carl Rosa Opera Company 1916-1924, Eva Turner made her Proms debut in 1934. She had a fine, clear voice of full tone and she is remembered 'for soaring over the whole orchestra on Wagner Night.'

In 1938 she had a chance meeting with Wood at Paddington Station and he asked her to sing in a Jubilee concert. She replied that she would be able to manage 'a cough and a spit.' She never forgot she was a Lancashire lass - albeit one who became admired and loved the world over, particularly for her singing in the Mozart operas.

RALPH VAUGHAN WILLIAMS (1872 - 1958)

English composer who studied under Stanford, Bruch and Ravel. His music is expressive of the English character and nationality and the tradition of choral singing. His *Sea Symphony* (1910) was set to words by Walt Whitman and much of Vaughan Williams' subsequent work was based on folksongs. He conducted his *Tallis Fantasia* and *Pastoral Symphony* in Promenade concerts in the years immediately after the First World War.

27th September 1934 was designated Vaughan Williams Night. And in 1952 all his eight symphonies were given as a tribute to his eightieth birthday. Wood said that Vaughan Williams 'has beaten those striving-for-originality moderns at their own game.'

Vaughan Williams was admitted to the OM in 1935.

SIR WILLIAM WALTON (1902 - 1983)

One of the most outstanding of all British composers, largely self-taught. He was also a highly-cultivated and witty man. The Directors of the Three Choirs Festival once asked him for a composition and he sent them *Belshazzar's Feast*, his quite brilliant oratorio. The officials at Gloucester Cathedral sent it back, saying that it was not suitable for playing in a consecrated building. So he sent them back a copy of the Old Testament!

He conducted his Facade - a setting of Edith Sitwell's verse for reciter and instruments - at the Proms on 30th September 1933 and his march *Crown Imperial*, written for the Coronation of George VI, was performed in 1937.

Walton's *Viola Concerto* is a masterpiece of neo-classicalism and it was given its premier on 3rd October 1929 with Paul Hindemith as soloist. A seventieth birthday concert was conducted in his honour by Andre Previn.

The History Of The Proms Celebrating 100 Seasons

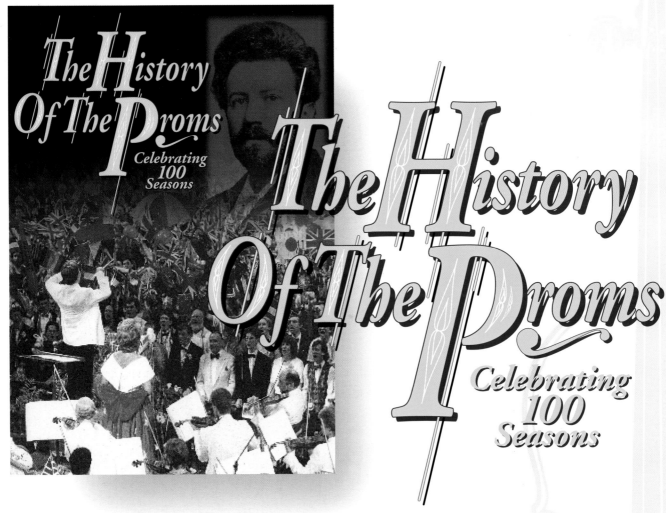

F urther copies of this book are available by writing to the publishers at the address below or by telephoning the order line. Requests for copies of the book to be sent as gifts will be despatched immediately. Please include with your order your full name and address, the full name and address of the recipient together with your cheque or postal order for £9.95 (incl p&p). All payments to: CMM Publications.
We hope that you enjoy your copy of the History of the Proms.

Please allow 7 days for delivery.

CMM Publications P.O.Box 547 High Wycombe Bucks HP12 4JJ
Telephone Order Line 0494 473069 / 473079
Mastercard & Visa cards accepted with telephone orders.